THEY MADE ME DO IT

Elle Benét

THEY MADE ME DO IT
Copyright © 2012 Elle Benét
All rights reserved.

No part of this publication may be reproduced, stored in a retrieval system, or transmitted in any form or by any means, electronic, mechanical, photocopying, recording, or otherwise, without written permission of the publisher.

ACKNOWLEDGEMENTS

The year 2010 was as though navigating through a thick fog – though unable to discern my comrades through the haze, they still made their presence known. For every time I faltered, there was a hand reaching out to elevate me...

It was you Jodie – as you fulfilled a role as my brother and father – and raised me the best way you knew how. And it was you Mike – who was there during all those times when it was tough for me to differentiate between the father/brother role of Joe... and for standing there as solely my brother, as someone I could talk to about things I would never share with a parent.

It was you Chrissy – who stood by me as my sister – I feel we have a true connection, and that we can relate to each other as both women and mothers.

To my siblings Eric and Jeff – it was you whom I thank for the moments of laughter that helped put a smile on my face during a rough day. To my mother in law, Natalie – it was you who offered a source of strength and support for which I am eternally grateful.

To my very close friends – many of whom I consider my sisters as well – Tabitha, Lisa, Christina, Glenda, Patti – it was you who provided me the continual support at the times I needed it most.

Indie and Nate – you are two angels that propel me to levels I never thought imaginable.

It was you who were my comrades throughout my journey and it is to you I dedicate this book.

INTRODUCTION

So why did I decide to use the title "They Made Me Do It?" The phrase – often heard in the singular: *he* made me do it, *she* made me do it – may remind many people of their school days. How many times have you heard a child use those words in an attempt to absolve themselves from a crime, whether it be an offence of a serious nature or a simple caught-with-hand-in-the-cookie-jar act of childhood naughtiness?

People do it all the time; it's much easier to blame others for the predicaments we find ourselves in than it is for us to wholly accept the responsibility for what we've done. For instance, it's easy to say, "I didn't know this would happen: *he* didn't give me all the facts," or "I got a bad grade because the *teacher* didn't explain the lesson to me properly," or "I never meant to do it, but *she* told me I had to." Blaming others for our own actions – especially actions that have the potential to get us into a lot of trouble – is not only tempting, but it is also universally practiced. No one, no matter where they come from or what their background is, likes to admit they're in the wrong, and we're usually all too quick to point the finger at anyone other than ourselves. It's a form of self-preservation, of saving face, of trying to appear to others as the best possible version of who we are.

It does, however, get to the point where we need to change our way of thinking. We can't blame every aspect of our lives on the actions – wrong or otherwise – of other people. Instead of externalizing the blame, we have to start looking a little closer to home; we have to accept that the person who has the most control over our destiny is us. No one else has as much power over the way we live our lives, or the way things turn out, as we do. Sometimes we have to take responsibility for our actions, and this doesn't necessarily have to be a bad thing; it can, for instance, show a great strength of character. Admitting we are wrong, or that we are at fault, doesn't come naturally to most of us.

Even if others are – partially or wholly, indirectly or directly – to blame for some aspect of your life, it is not the circumstances you find yourself in, but how you deal with the situation – and with the idea of blame – that defines who you are as a person. In my life, blame is an idea that has always been present (even if I didn't realize it at the time), and I've learned that it isn't necessarily about knowing where to place the blame, but about knowing where *not* to. Blaming others for the way your life has panned out is not only unhealthy, but extremely narrow minded; at times, you have to take responsibility for yourself and for your own actions, no matter how hard it is to admit.

When looking back on my past, I often find myself wondering, "how did I get here?" With all the negative experiences and all the pain and hurt that I've lived through, it would be all too easy to blame other people for everything that has happened to me – and the ones I love – in my life, and yet, I feel no need to start throwing any kind of blame around.

Instead, I choose to credit these people: without everything I went through when I was growing up, as well as the more recent events of my life, I wouldn't be who I am today. The experiences I've had and the people I've encountered along the way have contributed to the strong, healthy, happy individual I am now. Whether knowingly or not (and usually, it's 'not'), they have made me a better person. Why would I blame them for that?

So, considering that I have chosen not to blame those around me for the way my life has turned out, why did I want to write this book? I know there may be other people out there who are able to relate to my story – even if in a small, seemingly insignificant way – and some of those people may well be saying those five words, 'they made me do it,' as an excuse for the way they've lived their lives. I'm here to show you that it doesn't have to be that way: the things that other people do and say can shape us more than we could ever think possible, and this can be a very good thing. If you'd had an easier upbringing, a simpler life – with no trials and tribulations to get through – would you be the same person you are today? Forgetting about blame and focusing instead on giving others credit for the role they've played in your life can be therapeutic, too. How liberating would it be to not only forgive the people you've been blaming for your situation, but to acknowledge the vital role that they've played in your existence? Even thank them for what they've done for you?

Why not try and find some good in the past and use it to better your future? It's what I've done, and it's what I continue to do as I start each new morning and see what life has ready to throw at me today – both the good and the bad. The things I went through in my childhood, while extremely hard at the time, ultimately prepared me for everything that has come my way since. My childhood was a good life practice, an invaluable rehearsal for my adult years.

I once came across this statement: "Don't look back – you're not going that way." While this is good advice in some respects, I'd argue that although you may not be *going* that way now, it can still be a useful path to follow when considering your future. After all, if we don't look back from time to time, we'll never see how far we've come, and that, essentially, is what I'd like to get across in these pages: no matter what our background, we should never forget where we've come from, and in using this book to delve into my past and show you how I've benefited from it rather than been harmed by it, I'll never forget my origins. I wouldn't want to. I hope you never forget where you come from, either. After all, it is a part of ourselves: it always has been, and it always will be. The path we have been made to walk has made us who we are today.

I said that 'they made me do it' was a typical childhood phrase. Well, my childhood was a little different from most, but even with everything I've been through, I just can't bring myself to blame *anyone* for it. Instead, I'll use this book to thank the people who have, – in some way or other – had an impact on my life: they made me do it, but they don't deserve any blame for this. There's just too much to be grateful for, too much to live for. Yes, they made me do it: they made me become the person I am today. And I am immensely proud of that person.

I have seen far too many things while walking along my path to throw everything away on blame or bitterness. Instead, I want to digest everything that happened in my life, to learn from the experiences I had, and to move on – taking them all with me on the next section of my journey, whatever that turns out to be.

But in order to do that, I have to go right back to the beginning, to the very start of my path.

Dear Mom,

I want to say I'm sorry for any and all the pain I caused – but I only wanted to be the person you were afraid of being. I wanted to show you there are no repercussions for enjoying life. You didn't have to hurt every day and be a martyr in order to reap a reward in heaven. Heaven is here, Mom. Heaven is what you make your life to be and, when you die, I promise you it only gets better. And, since we couldn't talk… I was only trying to show you that by the only means I knew – by living it for you to witness. Even though you are not physically here, I know you are witnessing all of this. I feel you are still watching over me and the way I live my life. I feel that you see how I am raising the grandchildren I wish you could meet.

You always told me that we have to show people we are different by dressing differently. But I think you got wrapped up in the wrong thing – because our clothes are merely used to cover our bodies, but they fail to mask what is truly in our hearts.

With deep appreciation,

Your daughter

PROLOGUE

I'm sitting in the dark. There are no windows, no discernible sounds or other distractions, nothing left to do but contemplate the things that happened to get me here. In an abstract sense, there are many people who could be held responsible for my current situation — they made me do it.

But it's okay; I'm calm now — confident. I have my control back. I know it's only a matter of time before it's over and I will be free. In fact, there is no doubt in my mind that by the time I have finished writing these excerpts for the whole world to read, I will be free. It's only a matter of time. That's all it ever is, in the end. It's all about time, and belief.

I keep thinking about my life and now, some of it doesn't seem real. Thinking back over everything that's happened, running the thoughts over and over in my head, it sounds like one of those stories that happen to someone else, or a movie, maybe. Sometimes I think it might be, but sitting here, with an absence of light and anything else to muddy my thoughts, I know that it was all real. Some memories might be jumbled, my timeline might not be perfect, but I know if I concentrate hard, I can make some sense out of the things that happened to get me here. Sometimes the truth can be almost unbelievable, but I am certain that I can pick my way through it and find the meaning at its center.

I clench my fists against my leg and think about where to begin.

CHAPTER ONE

The purpose of this book isn't to evoke sympathy or horror at the things that have happened in my life. It isn't a tract designed to rail against events that have already happened or a vessel in which to hold an outpouring of grief. Well. I suppose, on some level, it is all of those things, but it's much more than that, too – at least I sincerely hope it will be. I hope that this book will be useful to someone. I hope that it will do them some good, in the same way that I hope the cathartic experience of collecting together my memories and writing them down will do *me* some good. I'm writing this book as a testament to the resilience of human nature and to show what can be achieved, despite the fact that even trying can sometimes seem so hopeless. We always prevail, somehow, and there is always something good to take from every situation. There is always hope; you just have to know how to look for it.

They say that whatever doesn't kill you makes you stronger and, while it might be a cliché to say it, it's also a cliché for a reason. There's a truth in there that can be inspiring: as long as we are alive, we can grow and become better, stronger people. There are things that have happened in my life that I suppose would have justified my giving up and giving in, but pushing through and carrying on has made me come out as a better, fuller, stronger individual on the other side. Pushing through hasn't always been fun or easy, but it has always been worth it in the end. There is always something to live for, I suppose is what I'm trying to say. Even if it doesn't always seem like it at the time.

I was born and brought up in a cult. I spent the first 18 or 19 years of my life there – it's hard to pinpoint exactly how long it was as so much of that time seems like a blur to me now and there are so many things which I would really rather just forget. But I did spend my whole childhood there and things that happen in your childhood always affect you later on in your life – even if you hardly remember much of it. Whatever kind of upbringing you have, it shapes you. It influences you, for better or worse. There's no way it can't. I'd say that's certainly true of me; growing up in this strict religious community shaped me as a person even if the life I live now couldn't be further from how I lived my early years. This book isn't so much about my life in the cult as how it has got me to where I am today, so it will only form a part of my writing, albeit an important one.

Instead of focusing on the difficult years of my upbringing, I want to concentrate on the good things that have come out of them, as I can now look back and understand that the positives in my life have far outweighed the negatives. I may not have been able to see it at as a teenager, but with age (even for someone still young like I am), comes perspective, and an appreciation for things that may have previously seemed like the worst thing in the world. Now that I'm out of my childhood years and away from my less-than-conventional upbringing, I can stand back and be thankful for the things it taught me as well as the other things I took from it: the lessons I went on to learn on my own.

I won't give the name of the religious organization because I don't want them to be inundated with media attention or scrutiny, but I don't think it's too much to say that it was a relatively small community. It was – and still is – based in Philadelphia, with offshoots in places including Africa and Mechanicsburg. There were probably a few hundred people who were members while I was there and it was a largely closed community: a proper 'them and us' situation. This strict segregation didn't change the entire time I was growing up in Philadelphia, but my views on it certainly did. As I said, with age comes perspective, and with perspective comes a new understanding of the world.

It sounds so weird to say 'cult'. You say the word 'cult' and it sounds like something that's a secret, hidden, kept largely from view. I guess in a way it was – the community was extremely reluctant to admit newcomers and even people who were desperate to join us were treated with suspicion. 'Outsiders' were exactly that, and I learned of the obvious 'them and us' divide from a very young age. So much happened behind closed doors that the world never saw, yet at the same time, the lives we lived were there for everyone to see. It could have been any ordinary-looking street in practically almost any ordinary-looking place in America – on the face of it. It's been one of the biggest lessons of my life that 'the face of it' is often very different to what's hidden underneath. If you start digging below the surface, all kinds of things come to light.

At first glance, this sounds ominous, but over time I've come to think that there's a lot of good in what's underneath the surface. Apparently, the icebergs that we see breaking through the surface of the ocean are only one eighth visible to us above the water – most of their mass is hidden from sight below the waves. Of course, this means that there's the possibility for hidden danger in our lives as well as in nature, but it also means that we have a huge amount of hidden strength, possibilities and potential – and that is by no means a bad thing. We can't always see what we might be able to achieve, but that doesn't mean we don't have the opportunity or the ability within us to do just that. This wasn't exactly something I was taught when I was a young girl growing up in the community, but it is definitely something I have learned for myself since.

But I digress. For the first years of my life, I didn't notice that anything was odd or out of place with my situation.

You don't, really, when you're that young. In a lot of ways, my childhood (before I started questioning things), was a happy one – at least in terms of practicalities. We lived in an affluent area and my parents' house would be a dream property to many; it was a three story, stone building with four bedrooms and a large yard. My father spent a lot of his time outdoors gardening and looking after the lawn, and my mother arranged her potted plants in a large bay window in the living room. There was another window on the other side of the room through which you could see the lawn and the results of my father's yard work; I loved looking out at the beautiful flowers – such as roses – that filled the air with their delicious scent. Our piano was placed next to this window and in the summer my brothers and I would practice our classical pieces while feeling the refreshing breeze floating through the open window. To some, this might sound idyllic, but as I grew up I started focusing less on our gorgeous home and more on what was happening around me.

As a child, you have no better information to go on than the world immediately surrounding you, and what your parents and other family members tell you, so it was quite some time before I started to think that maybe the cult didn't exactly operate on a normal level, if there is such a thing as 'normal'. You simply accept the way life is when you're being brought up by someone else: it doesn't even enter a child's mind to question it. Why would it? I lived with my mother, my father and four brothers – three of them older than me and one younger. I was never allowed to associate with children from outside the cult, but that seemed entirely normal to me. We had never known anything else. It was just what happened in our community: it was the norm for us.

There were other things, too, that to most people would seem wrong or at least a little bit strange, but that to me and the other children around me were simply facts of life, just the way things were. Two relatively minor things that have nonetheless stuck with me over the years is the way that girls were not allowed to wear skirts that ended even one inch above the knee, and that they were required to pin up their hair before going into school. The thinking behind this was that some 'rebel' girls used to trim their hair, which wasn't allowed, so following that it always had to be pinned to hide the ends. It's often the relatively small things like this that seem the most absurd to me now, but then it's surprising how much control it is possible to exercise over someone simply by dictating how they wear their hair and how they dress.

Controlling someone's appearance goes hand in hand with controlling their personality and their ability to express themselves through how they look. In this regard, all the girls were pretty much the same – we had no makeup to distinguish ourselves, no jewelry to adorn our necks or our ears, and even things like nail polish weren't allowed. As well as dictating the length of our skirts, the types of dresses and shirts we owned were controlled, too: we couldn't wear anything that was deemed to be 'revealing' in any way. Women in the cult were not allowed to wear slacks or pants, and we had to put on a hat when entering church. I remember going swimming and not being permitted to wear a bathing suit; I had to wear a dress, instead. Men generally wore shirts and jeans (or a different style of pant), but were expected to wear suits or dress pants to church.

As a young girl, I felt that my clothing choices were more controlled than others, as some girls my age could choose to wear more revealing things; some parents, for example, would allow their daughters to wear shorts. Those day to day things, they're more important than we might at first think. When I was younger, I simply didn't understand the rules about clothing, especially the divide between the sexes. I once got curious enough to ask my mother why women couldn't wear pants. The answer I received wasn't satisfactory at all; I was only told I had to 'simply obey' the rules. Like with many things in life, it was all about power.

Although we didn't know it at the time, every single aspect of our lives was controlled by an authority figure – in the case of families in the cult, this was the father. As children, we had no freedom to do exactly what we wanted (we couldn't, for instance, strike up a conversation with someone outside of our community, couldn't try and make friends with anyone who wasn't part of the cult). Our upbringing was strict, our rules confining. Our childhoods were controlled by people who had great power over us. It is in escaping this type of ruling that gives us freedom, but as young children, we had no concept of our confinement. We simply accepted it as the way things were meant to be.

The power in the cult was also represented in the significance played by religion. Not all cults are based on religion – all it takes is a specific, strong, unshakeable belief in *something* – but ours was heavily focused on God. Religious services were held multiple times a week: Monday evening, Tuesday morning, Wednesday evening, Saturday evening, Sunday morning, Sunday afternoon and Sunday evening. They formed much of the structure of cult life: they had to, really, with so many of them. It was practically impossible to live your life without organizing it around those services – not that it occurred to many young people to try.

The services took place in the church, which was connected to the school. The church building was a very large, stone structure with three levels: a basement, the main floor, and the balcony. The whole of the main floor could be overlooked from up on the balcony, and it was on the main floor of the building where the preacher held most of the services. I spent a long time during my childhood in that church, listening to the preacher teach us all about God as well as telling us who in the community needed praying for, whether it be because of an illness they were suffering through or a prayer that was needed for someone who was struggling to stay strong for one reason or another.

The main floor of the church was similar, I suppose, to many others: there were pews where we sat down to listen to the services, and they were all covered in a red cloth-like material. The sides of the pews were made from a dark wood which matched the dark wood of the beautiful altar. The preacher's semicircular podium was set behind this altar, and it was from there he'd deliver his sermon. Behind the podium stood a large raised platform made for the purpose of a choir, though its only use was when the children put on Church Christmas plays or held Graduation ceremonies.

I remember the extremely large brass organ pipes that were situated in the choir section; they were so tall and wide, they seemed to take up the whole view of that end of the church.

The basement of the building also consisted of many seats for the congregation, but they weren't the same as the pews in the main hall: they were simple, wooden, fold-up chairs which were divided into three different sections. The balcony level did, however, contain the same dark wood and red cloth pews that were present in the main hall, and which could be seen from the vantage point upstairs.

The church was connected to the school building, which was pretty similar to most other school buildings; at least, it had a normal classroom setting. At the beginning of each marking period new seating arrangements were assigned by the teachers which the students, usually begrudgingly, sat for the duration of that period. I remember having to line up when it was time to switch classes; we weren't allowed to go to our next lesson until we'd formed a neat, tidy line. We had to walk quietly down the hall to our next class to avoid disturbing other classes that may have still been in session. As to be expected, lunchtime was the highlight of the day. Kids went and seated themselves with their friends, pulling up their seats to form a little circle. Then the lunch swapping would begin- chips being traded for a candy bar, a grape juice box traded for an apple. When the bartering ended and everyone was satisfied we hurriedly ate so we could run outside and play. Outside activities were held in the parking lot. There wasn't any grass to sit on, but we did play games such as four square, basketball, and football (for the boys).

While the school was typical of many other American learning practices, the practices of the church were definitely not typical: the sheer amount of religious services that we had to attend is just one example. The church services could be extremely repetitive - something which became harder to stomach, the older I got. They consisted of a sermon, hymns, and then prayers to end with – all together lasting for an hour. These services were very similar throughout the week except for Sunday. Sunday was consumed with three different church events and in this way, the vast majority of the day was taken up with religious services and learning. The morning service was like those in the week – an hour of sermon, hymns and prayers. After this, we could go home and relax for a while with our families. We'd just have time for a quick meal and then we'd have to head back for Sunday school: this started at 2:30pm and again lasted for an hour. Sunday school lessons basically consisted of the children listening to the teachers while sitting quietly – divided up – in our age groups. After this, we could again go home for some more relaxation. Every afternoon we'd pick up the Sunday paper on the way home, so we could sit and read it while we had some spare time. Well, my father read through the paper; my brother and I would look at the comics while our mother cooked the dinner. In order to relax, we took off our church clothes, only to have to put them back on after dinner – ready for the evening service. This started at 7:30pm and ran in a similar vein to the others. After it had ended, we'd stand in the parking lot and talk to our friends before heading home.

The services weren't exactly my favorite part of the day; not only were they relatively boring to someone so young, but they happened so frequently and consisted of the same structure every time that they became increasingly difficult to sit through. They became even harder to attend when I got old enough to start questioning things – I'm inquisitive by nature but like with many things in the cult, I wasn't supposed to question authority. I received the same answer to my questions about religion as I'd got to my questions about clothes: I had to simply obey. That was it. I often got the feeling that my parents themselves didn't completely understand everything that was being taught to us in the services, but – as I was supposed to do – they simply obeyed.

We did, however, try and make the best of all the church services – in any way we could. I still have a fond memory of looking over at my brother as he concentrated his full attention on his hymn book throughout the service. I was impressed until I realized that he was hiding one of his novels inside the hymn book, using the religious cover as a kind of disguise. This got to be a regular occurrence with him, and I'm sure he learned a lot during all of the services he attended – just not from listening to the preacher. In an odd way, I think that all of this made faith ultimately mean less.

The services made it a routine, not a passion- something that must be completed simply because you are told to do it, much like homework or an undesirable household chore. Religion, or a belief of any kind, is a very personal thing. People can preach and indoctrinate you all they want, but at the end of it all, your mind is still your own. All the religious services in the world couldn't convert you as long as you have the strength and clarity of your own convictions. You still have your own thoughts. I understand that this isn't always true, but for me it certainly was; I was always able to think for myself and I'm grateful for that freedom. If it wasn't for that fact, I wouldn't be here right now, writing down my thoughts and memories for this book. A lot of people think that if you live in a cult and hear religious messages all the time, then you must become convinced by it all and believe in it absolutely. I think it's a testament to the hidden strengths of individuals that this isn't always necessarily the case. These days, I'm very spiritual, but religion doesn't play much of a part in my life – it's a personal choice, and one I'm very proud I'm able to make. The chance to decide for myself isn't something I ever thought I'd have, and I make sure I don't take the opportunity for granted.

Part of the religion of the cult I grew up in was that cult members were not allowed to visit a doctor. If you were ill – even if you were dying – it simply meant that it was your time to go. One of my early childhood memories is of an illness that was going round the community: measles – which is a completely treatable childhood disease – was quickly spreading around the cult's children (one thing that most people know about measles is that it is highly contagious). Despite the fact that it was treatable, due to the lack of medical care, children were actually dying because of it. When untreated, measles can lead to encephalitis and pneumonia, which can be fatal, and that's what started happening in our small community. It's hard to think about it now, and it's certainly hard to write it down in this book, but I was young and – as it was the norm – I simply didn't question it. I didn't know that there was any other way of living. People dying – even children – was just a matter of course. It was horrible, but it was natural. Or so it seemed to me then.

One of those unfortunate children was my cousin. I was about seven years old at the time and I remember seeing her in school one day… and then I simply never saw her again. It was years before I found out that she had died from a curable illness – her and many others. The spate of deaths even brought a TV crew to the community; I have a vivid memory of sitting on a couch with my parents while they were questioned by the crew. I didn't, however, grasp why the TV people were there. Later, someone told me 'Look! Your house is on TV!' At the time, I thought it was really cool. It was only later that I realized the true reason for them being there and the very significance of it.

The measles incident – while clearly foremost in my mind because it happened when I was part of the cult – was by no means the first time the community had attracted controversial news coverage due to its practices. Outsiders just couldn't understand why otherwise loving and devoted parents would let their own children die – simply because they believed in the healing power of God – and that, if a child died, it was because of His will. Seeking medical help showed a lack of trust and a lack of faith and was therefore a sin. Other children and teenagers had died from a variety of treatable diseases over the years, and this inevitably led to court cases and vast media exposure (I wasn't aware of this then; I have found it all out since).

Some parents – who had lost a son or a daughter – were charged with involuntary manslaughter, but it was the measles case that really angered outsiders: it wasn't just that a number of children had died (which, of course, is bad enough in itself), the problem was also with the rest of the children who attended the community's school. They had not been immunized against the disease, and therefore kids who'd never come into contact with measles before were at a high risk of contracting it. And – without the proper medical care they would require – they, too, could die from the completely curable disease. Outsiders simply couldn't accept this; they couldn't understand why it was being allowed to happen.

But happen, it did. It was against the community's religion to immunize against any threat to their health, showing that it wasn't just medical cures they refused to accept; it was disease prevention as well. The offered inoculations – and therefore the offer of life – were turned down by the school, as it would be against God's will.

It wasn't just the deaths of young children that horrified outsiders, though: it was the way their parents seemed to simply accept that this was meant to happen. They thought it was just meant to be. It was normal to us in the cult, but no one else could comprehend the reasons behind it. Wouldn't God want to help his followers in any way he could? Didn't he send talented people to Earth to become doctors so they could heal their fellow men and women? How can it be God's will to allow a whole group of children to die from something that is so easily prevented? Of course, I wasn't aware of any of this then; I had no idea how many times the community had been chastised for its beliefs about life and death, had no grasp of what the meaning behind the TV crew was when they came to interview my parents. I was too young to put two and two together, still too much a part of the cult to even think of looking at things from a different perspective.

The other way that cult members looked at the deaths – particularly the child deaths – was that, as it was God's will, and he knows more about our lives than we do on Earth, the deaths would have been for a reason. This reason could be bringing families – and the rest of the community – together, making them stronger, or it could have been seen as a lesson: a death in the family will make you appreciate everything else you have that much more. Instead of focusing on material things or petty arguments, a death will focus you back on religion and make you concentrate more on God. Many of the community members believed that disease and the death of a loved one could be explained as being due to something wrong in their own lives, something that needed changing or improving, such as their relationship to others or their relationship with God. It was thought that everything happened for a reason, you just had to look hard to find out exactly *which* reason.

Because the deaths (in the case of the measles) were those of children, the uproar in the media was understandably much worse than it would have been if they'd been adults: children – especially young ones – don't have the option to choose a hospital over their religion. Adults, if they were really sick, could decide to disobey their community's rules and get medical help, if they were really desperate. The children weren't even aware that this was an option, and in any case, they would have been too young to try and get medical attention by themselves. They were helpless; victims of their parents' beliefs, not able to decide their fates for themselves. This is what got the media so riled up, this is why there was such controversy over the deaths. It just seemed like far too high a price to pay for pleasing God.

It was incidences like this that started the whole idea of calling our community a 'cult'. The word can mean a lot of different things to different people, and it can conjure up a whole range of stereotypical ideas, including horrific notions like suicide pacts. The community I grew up in was nothing like that, but the media – the TV crews, the news stations, the local publications – didn't know what else to call us. We certainly weren't 'normal' in their eyes, just as outsiders weren't 'normal' to many of the community members. We held what could be seen as opposing beliefs, we lived our lives in different ways, and we had a much stricter structure in terms of how children should grow up. Society in general doesn't like things that are different, or things that they can't understand. So we got labeled as a 'cult,' and while it is a pretty strong word for what our community was, it's as good a word as any to use when describing my time there.

I wish I had known at the time why my cousin and the others had all died. I think about it a lot even now; it's simply not the kind of thing you ever forget. Death – when it could have been prevented – is horrible enough, but when the victims are children, it's almost incomprehensible. I feel as though I could have saved her if I had known, but I was never given the chance. I didn't have all the facts. No one my age did.

Around the same time, one of my older brothers also became really ill. He was essentially dying in the next room while the TV crew was interviewing my mother and father, a thought which is almost too awful for words. My brothers have always been my support network, and I remember being so scared he was going to die that I could hardly breathe. For days, I watched him get sicker and sicker. He kept getting thinner until he was practically skeletal. His eyes were sinking back into their sockets. He genuinely looked like a skeleton and I will never, ever be able to block out those images (it's always the single, striking images that stay with you from childhood, isn't it? Whole events – months, even – can be lost in the recesses of your mind and yet there are some things you can never shake, even if you try). The memory of my skeletal brother with his sunken eyes stays with me to this day.

After a few days of my brother being sick, there was a huge amount of commotion in the house. One of my older brothers had waited until our dad had gone to work and then he had taken our sick brother to the emergency room on his own: he had been waiting until there was no one around to stop him. It was the only way he could have done it. He told me later that there was just no way he could have let our brother die; he said he couldn't focus at work with his sibling being so sick and that he didn't care about the repercussions of getting him medical treatment. Of course, he was right. To deny a child medical care because of a belief they were never given a choice about is wrong. But, of course, the cult didn't see it like that. To them, everything was black and white, wrong and right. And to my father and the rest of the community, hospitals – and the medical profession in general – were most certainly wrong.

I remember that my mom was in distress, crying because my brother was in the hospital and it was against their religion to take him there. I remember my father rushing home from work as soon as he found out what had happened. I also remember my older brother telling me afterwards that, if he hadn't got our brother to the hospital when he did, he would have been dead within hours. There was something blocking his throat, preventing him from swallowing water even with the help of a dropper and, if the doctors hadn't burst it when they did, he would certainly have died. The thought is a truly chilling one.

It was one of the scariest and most intense moments of my childhood; the thought that my brother might die, the thought of what might happen as a result of my older brother taking him for help, and the potential that it had to have a huge impact on our family. Now, though, I just have to think about how grateful I am that he didn't die. It doesn't do to dwell on what might have been. The here and now – and the possibilities that are still to come – are far more important than events that have already happened. My brother lived. He was strong enough, and he got the help that he needed just in time. He lived. That's the most important thing to take from this whole incident.

There are some memories that are harder to write about than others, and the brutal beatings my brothers endured are most definitely one of them. The abuse was a part of what went on in our household, much the same as refusing medical treatment and all the other number of things we did that seemed so normal at the time but seem so horrific now. My brothers and I weren't supposed to talk about them with anyone outside of our home, but I now realize that doing so would not have been the wrong measure to take. These were things that went on behind closed doors and, as far as home life was concerned, that is where they were supposed to stay. Yet we would have been completely within our rights to get outside help. These beatings occurred constantly and at times unexpected… they weren't just a light tap on the buttocks or the occasional swipe of a belt. It was physical abuse, pure and simple.

To live in that sort of environment, with the threat of a beating weighing your choices and decisions, is extremely unnerving, especially for a child whose intentions are generally agreeable. After all, your parents are in a position of authority, a position of trust. It's part of their role to keep you in line, and to raise you how they think best. It's sometimes difficult for a young mind to comprehend that something is really, truly wrong, and even when we all knew how wrong it was, to know what to do about it was another challenge that was hard to overcome. When it's all you've known throughout your childhood, knowing how to change it isn't easy.

Despite not being aware of much outside of our community, I knew inherently that these beatings were wrong. One memory – out of all the terrible things that happened during those beatings – has stayed with me to this day: the images of my mom crying refuse to leave my mind, no matter how much I wish they would go away.

Now that I am older, I think I can understand much better the pain my mother must have gone through while we were growing up. I suppose it's fair to say that while my father was a 'father' to us, he wasn't really a 'dad' in all the ways he could have been, or should have been in the mind of a young girl. I can't recall any occasion where he spent any one-on-one time with me... whether it was simply rocking me to sleep, reading me a book, or just helping me with my homework. It just wasn't what he did or who he was; he didn't engage with his children on that level, and that was normal to him. My mom was essentially bringing up five children on her own and she was basically just trying to hold the family together. On top of that – no matter what happened – if you lived in the cult, there was no way you were ever to leave your spouse. It just wasn't done. So she didn't do it.

ELLE BENÉT

As is true in a rather scary number of cultures, the men were undeniably in charge: they always got their way and challenging their decision was, to say the least, inadvisable. Inadvisable, and at times, dangerous.

Sometimes, girls in the cult would be molested by their cousins, brothers, fathers... It didn't happen to everyone, and it certainly wasn't the norm, but it *was* something that happened in the community – and the structure of the cult gave the molesters a cloak to hide behind. It often seemed as though there was no act so malicious that it couldn't be atoned for and healed through prayer. These acts that took place, they were only ever whispered about. It was all very hush hush, always covered up. The repercussions were not as they should have been: a prayer was all there was. That was the only consequence of an incident as horrific as that. The general feeling seemed to be that if no one said anything about the problem, it didn't exist in the first place. Out of sight, out of mind. It's a bit like that old conundrum: if a tree falls in the woods but no one is there to hear it, does it make a sound? Was everything that happened really real if nothing was ever said about it? All I know is that, in the cult, whatever the man said, stood. There was just no other way.

Sometimes, I feel a little bit cheated. While the cult had its own school, which combined grade and high school in the same building, further education was frowned upon. I wanted to go to college. I remember one instance when I wanted my parents to sign some forms so I could get a loan to go and continue with my studies, but they wouldn't do it. It all came back to power again: I was being controlled by my parents, and in particular, my father, who had total power over me. There was nothing I could have done to change his mind. I feel a little bit like I missed out, not getting that part of my education.

Then I remember that I've learned far more from the 'university of life' and have experienced so much in the ensuing years – and achieved so much, as well – that really, it's okay. I might not have a bunch of letters after my name, but I have something (while less tangible), is altogether more important than that. It would have been nice to go to college but I wouldn't say that not going has held me back in any way. Only you can hold yourself back, and I'm determined to never do that. There are too many things I want to achieve to even consider not trying.

When it came to schooling in the cult, only children from our enclosed community were permitted to attend. If you were not part of our congregation and didn't follow our rules or share our beliefs, then your children were not allowed at the school. This cold attitude permeated other parts of cult life, from not being welcoming to newcomers to the acts that happened behind closed doors and were never talked about.

Other things, too, that it's so easy to take for granted now, were not allowed then. For instance, the only music we were allowed to play and listen to was hymns. We weren't allowed to dance, either: it was more or less forbidden. I chuckle now, reflecting back on one memory in particular:

It's Christmas and our family has just arrived home from an evening church service. I am keen to change out of my church clothes, so I race upstairs as fast as I can, knowing that the quicker I am, the sooner I'll be able to get to the kitchen and start baking holiday treats – cookies and other delicious snacks. After I've changed my clothes, I run back to the stairs but realize I've left my newest prized possession on my bed. It's a cassette that plays both radio and tapes, and I run back to retrieve it. It's my little secret. Something that's my very own. Just for me. We have always been taught against radio and television within the community, and so the cassette radio is my illicit treasure. I have slipped in a tape of hymns just in case my parents ask to hear what I am listening to. I at least know to do that much.

I place the headphones over my ears and flip the dial to 'radio'. A 'worldly' song is playing, and the beat of it encourages me to move and bob my head along to it. I go back downstairs and get out the ingredients I will need to bake. Mom is bustling about in the kitchen, busy whipping up her own treats for Christmas. It's a nice time in our house; there's a good feeling of energy in the air.

I smile to myself — no one is the wiser about what I am listening to. The thought that I have my own secret is extremely satisfactory. And then one of my favorite songs comes on. I lose myself in the music and can't help but move along to it: I'm swaying my hips, smiling, rocking my head and getting my dance on. I don't get to do this often enough. I hardly even know I'm doing it. I love it. Really love it. I'm lost in the music and I hardly notice when —

"Elle!"

"Elle!"

"Eleanora!"

I freeze. I am so caught. I sheepishly remove my headphones and look at my mother. She's standing watching me, her hands on her hips. "Don't you dare move your body in that manner!" she says. "You know better than that."

Then her eyes soften. She says nothing further and returns to her baking.

Immediately, I feel terrible. Not just for expressing myself, but for disappointing my mom. I look at my cassette player and sigh. She's right: I knew better than that.

In fact, I wasn't allowed to associate with them at all. It was this strict rule of my childhood that led to such problems later on in my life.

It might have seemed normal at the time, but looking back I can see how restrictive it was, how comparatively lonely it was. I suppose it was to try and stop me and the other children from being swayed by the beliefs of others, by their different lifestyles and ways of worshipping – or not worshipping – a certain religion. I'm not sure whether they were intentionally trying to limit our childhoods and all the experiences that should go with it, but in keeping us confined in such a narrow way of living, that was the ultimate result. I guess the adults hoped that if we didn't interact with anyone else, it would never occur to us to be anything other than members of the cult, following the rules and taking part in the community that was built up around it. It would never occur to us that the basic rules we lived our lives by might actually be wrong. I suppose it was like a family business, in a way, passing on skills and beliefs to the next generation, as happens right across the world and has done for millennia.

That theory didn't completely work, though. Growing up, I was always aware that there was something more to the world that existed outside of the cult. Once in a while a member would permanently leave, which was one of the grandest mistakes one could possibly make in the cult.

THEY MADE ME DO IT

The hope of their eternal salvation was crushed, for to seek any other course other than that which went against our teaching was an abomination in the sight of God. But my curiosity was always aroused by these occurrences. What was it like out there? Was it as terrible a place as the preacher said it was- "the path of unrighteousness"? Would there name be automatically blotted out of heaven because of this transgression?

That was the thing about the cult: everything took on a religious significance and anything that they wanted to hide, they shrouded in the guise of religion. It was a useful method, applying God and religion to explain away everything that happened in the community. It was convenient. The children are dying from some incurable disease? It's God's will. Parents standing trial on manslaughter charges for not providing their child(ren) with the medical attention needed? It means the end of time is near, that judgment day is coming and we have to be prepared to face the trials and tribulations that are sure to come with ever increasing frequency as the day draws near. It just means that we have to stay even more grounded in our faith and beliefs. We have to stick to the rules of the cult now more than ever. This is the purpose.

At least, this is the view they – the cult leaders – tried to present. In a way, their intentions were good. They genuinely believed what they were doing and they were trying to do right by their families and their faith. Unfortunately, the teachings were subjective as it was the preachers interpretation of the scriptures.

This led to people leaving the cult from time to time, particularly younger people who naturally wanted to make their own lives and their own way in the world, free from restrictions, free to think what they wanted, to do what they wanted, to see who they wanted. After all, it's only natural to be curious about what else is out there: it's human nature to want to learn and grow as a person. They say that when you're young, you're naturally more open to things, to new ideas and experiences, as it's in your interests to explore all the options – and to create new options – to find what's best for you. It's only as you get older that you become set in your ways and generally become more conservative, because at that point in life it's in your interests to preserve what you've got and to keep the status quo.

That's what I saw playing out in the cult, albeit in a much more tense, heightened setting than would normally be the case. The elders were trying to preserve what they had: they saw it as the only way to live and they wanted it to stay that way. They didn't like change of any kind. The young people and the others who left were looking for something more than what they had grown up with, so that when it came to their turn to be old, they could be proud of their own achievements. It's how the world works.

Even though it might not always seem like it, there is always something positive that can be taken from every situation. Sometimes the benefits might only be small, but they all add to our cache of life experiences and our store of things that are good about the world. It can take time for this to become clear; when we are caught up in the midst of a situation and can't quite see a way out, it can be hard to define the positive that exists within our lives. And yet it is always there – somewhere – and the gift that time and perspective have both given me is that I can now see just how much of my life has made me stronger. I'm incredibly proud of that.

Thinking about my upbringing in this way is a healthy exercise to do, not only for me but for anyone who has had a hard or troubled life. Violence and suppression are dark, dirty subjects that no one likes discussing or thinking too much about, but in taking note of these topics and how they affected me as a child, I can turn them into positive outcomes that now affect me as an adult – but in a completely different way. I am stronger for living through all of these things, and I now know I have the ability to take terrible memories from my past and turn them into something productive and actually useful for the future: both for my future and that of my children.

Not everyone who left the cult stayed away. The temptation for new things is juicy and bright, but at the same time, what you know is comforting. Quite a few who left eventually returned to the regimented way of life, because it was what they knew and it gave them security. A feeling of safety is incredibly important to a lot of people, and it is often placed above other – seemingly more important – things in life, such as excitement, happiness, and experiencing new things. That's okay, though. They gave it a go, tried a different way of living for a time, and were able to make a more informed decision about what they wanted to do as a result. That's important, I think – being properly informed. You can't know where you stand on an argument until you've heard more than one viewpoint and have tried to see things as other people see them. Of course, many others of the same age didn't leave; they simply didn't have all of the information they needed in order to make their decision. For many in the cult, information – like change – wasn't seen as a good thing: as I've already mentioned, education past school level wasn't exactly encouraged.

Others who left the cult found it hard to adjust on the outside. They tried to find coping mechanisms to get them through the hard times – drugs for some, alcohol for others. The fact is, you can say what you like about living in a cult (and I certainly would never go back), but it did provide a structure. It gave people a purpose and a way to arrange their lives. In that sense, it was an easy way to live.

It was a community. It had clear rules to follow. You didn't have to plan the rest of your life out or worry about what was coming next. Leaving that, going out into the world, often with nothing – nowhere to turn, no real sense of what to do, probably with no money, either – is very scary. There aren't strict rules out in the real world, there's no clear designated path to follow, and that can be a hard thing to accept when coming from a cult like the one I grew up in. The sudden abundance of choices is overwhelming, especially when compared to the very few choices that were available when living in the community. Too much variety and too much opportunity can be just as stifling to some people as too little, especially when they're not used to it. The people who left coped in any way they could. Some returned to cult life, some struggled on, some flourished. It was the act of trying to leave, trying to do something else with their lives, that struck me as being important.

In a weird way, I think it's a little bit like leaving for college: it's a time of transition and what you make of it can affect who you are for the rest of your life. Often, it's the first time a young person has lived away from home for any length of time, without the constant support of their parents and the family structure that they have grown up with. They're often in a location far away and, although they know that there's support for them at home – wherever that may be – they're all too aware that, for the first time, they're out there on their own. They've grown up and it's up to them to make the most of their chance, to make something of themselves. It can be daunting, and it affects different people in different ways: some give up and go home, back to what they know. Others drink and party, either as a way of rebelling or as a mask to hide their true insecurity. Sometimes, it's just to forget their day-to-day concerns. Others still thrive on it; the education and the freedom, the independence, the newness of it all, the opportunity to become something different, to become a successful human being away from the rules and confines of what they're used to. To many, it is a wonderful, liberating experience.

Leaving the cult was certainly an education for all who attempted it, no matter the outcome of their flight. I don't know why many of the people who had left had done it, but I can guess. Two of my own brothers left when I was around the age of 18. They had just gotten to the point with my father – with his temper, his beatings, the whole experience of him – that it had simply become too much. They had just had enough of it all. So they left. They just walked out the door and that was that.

I think that was part of what tipped me over the edge. It's all very well, hearing about the people who had left the cult and gone on to do new things with their lives, but until it happens to your own family, it's all a little bit abstract. It's perhaps something that is talked about, but never acted upon, at least not by anyone you really know well. I was aware that leaving was possible. I knew that walking out was always an option, but until my brothers did it, it wasn't a particularly tangible thing. It was always something that happened to other people. Suddenly, though, everything turned on its head. Something snapped inside me that said, *you know what? You don't have to put up with this*. It was as though they had brought everything that was never said, all those things we never spoke about, out into the light – not through words but through action.

That's important, I think. Words are powerful. They can hurt more than fists and inspire more than we can imagine. Words can be anything they want to be; language is amazing. But really, that's all it is. Words. Letters on a piece of paper or sounds coming out of someone's mouth. They can inspire a revolution but they can't actually *be* the revolution. That takes action. People have to carry through the sentiments inspired by the words and by the meaning behind them. My brothers had put action to the thoughts that must have been in so many of our heads and it was their decisiveness and bravery that gave me the courage for my own actions.

It was also appropriate. There was so much that we never said, and even when my brothers left, they didn't really say anything. They just did it.

THEY MADE ME DO IT

I'm not afraid of the dark. I've spent too much time in it to be scared of an absence of light. It's okay. The dark can be liberating; it hides us from others and gives us the privacy we sometimes need to be who we want to be. I'm going to be free soon. I know the way out. It's just a matter of time.

WHEN LIFE GIVES YOU LEMONS...

The past is the past and cannot be changed. It is this that makes me think I might as well glean something positive from my past experiences in the hope that they will help me to improve my future. It would be easy to be bitter about so much: bitter about the children who had died because they weren't given the medical help that they needed, and bitter about people found that they couldn't live in the outside world because the cult was all they knew. Bitter about being forced to live my life in a certain way, about being made to wear my hair in a certain style and my skirts at a certain length. Bitter about not being able to wear jewelry or express myself in any external way. Bitter about not being allowed to dance.

Some of these things make me deeply sad and probably always will, but to be bitter about them would be wasted energy that I could be using in a much more positive way. All I would achieve through bitterness and holding grudges is to hold myself back, and I don't want to punish myself for something over which I had no control, especially not now that things are so different. The people in my past wouldn't be affected by my bitterness; they most likely wouldn't even know how I truly felt. Most of them are still going about their lives as they see fit. I wouldn't achieve anything good by feeling like that, and I refuse to participate in an activity that will benefit no one.

So instead, from time to time, I like to engage in a little self-therapy to keep those negative feelings at bay. If I don't, I can sometimes sense them creeping up on me like a tide, threatening to sweep up and drag me back under. I don't want that. The energy I spend on focusing on the positive is more than worth it.

That doesn't mean that I ignore the negative things that have happened, or the negative things that I feel, but it does mean that I make the effort to reflect on the positive things I can take from them, as well as from all of the other events in my life. To take just one example to start with: my brothers being beaten throughout my childhood. This is undoubtedly a negative experience, and one that will always remain so. No one can argue that physical violence could ever be seen as anything else. My brothers – my own flesh and blood – were hurt when they shouldn't have been and I hate that they had to live through it all, hate that they had to put up with it so often when they could do nothing about it. Yet, believe it or not, there is still something positive to take from that time in our lives: I learned, for instance, that problems aren't solved by reacting in anger. To lash out in anger can build regrets in a person, and to live with regrets is never fun. One of the reasons my brothers left our childhood home is because even then, they realized that it would be wrong to hit back. To hurt our father in the way he had been hurting them – both physically and mentally – would just be fighting fire with fire, and since I've left the cult, I can really appreciate just how little that works, and how pointless it can ultimately be.

The experience has also helped me now, in my normal day-to-day living: it has shown me that this is not how I want to discipline and reprimand my own children. The last thing I want is for them to fear me in the way my brothers and I often feared our father. I want to be close to my children and have a good relationship with them, and that isn't something that can be achieved through violence. I have been given the opportunity to provide my children with an upbringing that I feel every child should have: a loving, caring, nurturing environment that encourages self-expression, encourages learning about other people and other ways of life, and encourages education and the opportunity to gain knowledge. When I think of my children's early years in comparison to mine, all of my sacrifices and hard work to get to where I am today seem incredibly worth it. They will get the chances that I – along with my brothers and friends – never had, and they will not be held back or be brought down by violence. Not ever.

Another negative experience from my childhood was the suppression that I experienced: I always had to contain how I felt. I had to watch what I said and be careful about what I wore. The important lesson I take from this is that a person's character cannot be determined by their articles of clothing; there is much more to us than that. Clothes might hide our bodies and our skin, but they will never hide who we really are, deep down inside. Although it might sound strange, I also think that learning to suppress what I say has helped me. It taught me how to get on and deal with things instead of wasting time on words that are unlikely to change anything; I probably would have sunk long before now if I didn't have that skill. It taught me that it isn't always wise to speak out – we have to choose our moments carefully, and use our words when they matter the most. It has also taught me independence and self-reliance, skills that have been invaluable to me since childhood.

CHAPTER TWO

Leaving the cult became inevitable once my brothers left. The longer I stayed there, the more I dreamed of what it would be like to leave and, now that I had the prospect of *somewhere* to go if I left, the temptation began to grow. It more or less took hold of me: I now had a connection with the outside world, and the possibility of exploring that world and everything that was contained in it gripped me. The thought of experiencing a different lifestyle – a freer, more tolerant style of living – helped to make me even more certain. I didn't want cult life anymore; I wanted options. I wanted freedom. I didn't decide to leave on a whim, without any thought, but once I *had* decided, I wouldn't let myself dwell on the decision. I couldn't allow myself to formulate any arguments that may have led to talking myself out of it. I knew my reasons for wanting to leave and I held onto them, tightly. It was time.

I think it's so important to always be able to justify your decisions – even if only to yourself – because you are ultimately the one who's going to have to live with whatever it is you decide. I didn't want any regrets, or to be asking myself 'why' in later life. I wanted to know that I had done the right thing, and for the right reasons, too:

luckily, my reasons for wanting to leave the cult couldn't have been any clearer.

Reason one was that I wanted to be with my brothers again; I missed them. They played a big part in raising me and I wanted to be near them; they are an important part of my life that I wouldn't do without. They were a link to my childhood, but to the good part of it, not the negative part. Reason two for leaving the cult was that I wanted to live my own life, away from the community, where I could develop my own beliefs and passions rather than living with those that were forced upon me. I wanted the freedom to explore my own mind and pursue any opportunities that I uncovered for myself, instead of always being told what to do and when. I was tired of following orders; I wanted to be the one to make my own decisions. And reason three for starting a new life was that I felt I needed some distance from my father. This was perhaps the biggest reason of all, and it was what ultimately helped me make up my mind to go.

It hurt me the way he seemed to devalue everything my mother did for the family and how he didn't seem to fully appreciate her. She was the one who basically held the family together: she ran the home and provided the love and care we so desperately needed, yet her contribution seemed to mean relatively little to him. This angered me, especially as I knew that couples in the cult weren't allowed to break up. There was no way out for her; there was never going to be a way out for her. It also caused me great pain to have to witness my brothers being whipped for some transgression or other. I didn't like to think that the man who was supposed to love and protect all of us was so willing to cause pain to his own children, his own flesh and blood. Clearly, my brothers had had enough of that, as well. This didn't particularly come as a surprise to me. I was getting to the same point of having enough myself.

I had also had enough of his lack of care and interest in me as a person, as an individual. I know that all parents are different and everyone has their own way of bringing up children – and rightly so, or else we'd all be the same and that would be boring – but one thing that all parents should have in common is love and interest in their kids, in particular an interest in helping them to develop their own personalities and supporting them to find their own direction and way in life. I still find it hard to deal with, years later: the fact that my father never seemed to get that I'm a person, too. He never wanted to know about my hobbies and passions. He never really took the time to talk to me, to find out what I thought about things, to seek out my opinion or simply my company. He never did any of the things that I thought a father should do. His interests lay in protecting the honor of the family: *his* honor. Everything was always about maintaining appearances. He didn't seem to care about what was underneath, or what should have been underneath. He only cared about how things looked on the surface: he merely concentrated on the tip of the iceberg, not what was beneath the water.

I felt like I was furniture in his life; something without feelings, that he sometimes casually rearranged to suit his own purposes and to make his own life more comfortable – something that was just there, rather than his child, who he should have naturally wanted to be involved with. An inanimate object rather than a daughter. It was that continual disinterest, punctuated only by moments of rage – on his part – that led me to my final tipping point.

There is always a tipping point, isn't there? It's amazing how much humans can put up with, on a regular basis and for so long, before finally, eventually, inevitably, something happens to push us over the edge and we have to take some kind of action. Sometimes we can't always identify what it is that has pushed us over the edge – we just know that something has, and that things cannot stay the same any longer. Something has to change, and it has to change now. It's amazing, though, just how often things *do* stay the same, despite the very best of intentions. That's the important point: intentions are crucial, but they do not create change within themselves. Things can't change unless we make them change. Otherwise, the moment of the tipping point will have been for nothing.

***THEY* MADE ME DO IT**

My advice would be to not ignore that moment when it comes. I didn't. It happens for a reason. I think it's a sign that enough is enough – a prompt that, actually, something has got to change and you need to do whatever you can to make that change happen. In my case, it was as though – for so long – everything had been precariously balancing on a knife edge, so delicate but still just about intact. There was plenty that was wrong, but there was nothing that really gave me a shove to do something about it – although part of that was fear, of course. Fear of the unknown, fear of change, fear of the repercussions in relation to what my father would do to me. Then the balance started to tip when my brothers left in quick succession of each other and the edge of that knife started to dig in. The fear of what might happen if I left the cult started to be taken over by the pain of staying – the balance started to tip. I felt myself beginning to be pulled more in one direction than the other and, from that point on, it was only ever a matter of time until I left. Nothing could dissuade me from my action.

How much time, exactly, was ultimately – if indirectly – decided by my father. There was one event in particular that just pushed me well and truly over the edge, and it acts as a reminder even now of just how different the two of us really are.

In the months leading up to my leaving the community, I had a job working for a gentleman who owned his own construction firm. He was a fellow cult member and I used to do general administration for him. The job itself was fine, but by this point I was itching to get out and meet people from the 'real world'; I'd had enough of living such a narrow existence and I really wanted to get away, to explore, to grow. Working for a cult member was just another sign of how insular the community was, and how closed down my options were when I thought of all the other things I could have been doing if I lived outside the cult. The possibilities in the real world were endless. Within the cult, possibilities didn't really exist at all. At least, not on the same level. If I wanted any chance of experiencing all of these wonderful opportunities, I simply had to leave. There was nothing else for it.

Clearly though, getting out and making new friends was never going to happen while I was living in that situation. Not only was it disallowed in the community, but the fact that I lived in a cult tended not to go down too well with the 'worldly' people I met. There is a certain stigma that comes with the notion of a strict religious organization, even though I was never one of the people who was truly committed to the cult's way of life. Sometimes it makes me sad the way we judge people, but it is unfortunately something that is as understandable as it is inevitable.

By the time it had become obvious that working for the construction firm was never going to get me the freedom and experiences I wanted, my second eldest brother had already left the house. He'd set himself up in a neighborhood a short distance away and was working as a personal trainer in a nearby gym. I asked him if there was any chance he could get me a job there, too. I knew it would be almost impossible to make it outside the cult without having a job lined up, and I was determined to have everything in place so that I could make a proper go of my new life as soon as I left. I wasn't about to jump headfirst into a completely unknown way of living without at least some kind of back up plan. This was a big step and, when my brother said yes – that he could help me get a job in the gym – I was unspeakably happy. For the first time, it seemed as though my dream might actually be achievable; a plan was beginning to take shape, and the thought that I could actually make it out in the world – without my parents – was incredibly exciting. It also set into motion the chain of events that led to me eventually leaving the cult – and my parents' house.

I knew that I was going to have to come clean about my plans. I'd prepared for the difficult conversation of telling my parents what I intended to do – but I hadn't prepared for the strength of my father's reaction when I told him that I had quit my job at the construction firm. I don't think it's an understatement to say that he was apoplectic. He just went mad when I told him: he was yelling and rampaging around the house, as angry as I'd ever seen him. This hadn't been what he'd wanted, and he never dealt with things well when they didn't go the way that he'd intended. After all, the head of the household was always the man, and the man was always right. To be challenged by one of his sons was bad enough, but to be challenged by his daughter as well… it made his reaction a hundred times worse.

It's not a nice feeling, seeing one of your parents in such a state because of something you've done. Especially when you know what they can do and have lived with the threat of it for your whole life. No one should have to live like that, yet far too many people do: it's something that affects people from all societies and backgrounds, and it's a problem we definitely need to take seriously. No matter what they tell you, or what you tell yourself in order to try and deal with it, it's never okay. There is never any excuse for physical violence or bullying of any kind.

I think my dad was embarrassed about me; he took his pride very seriously. He was dedicated to the way of life that was exalted by the cult and he was ashamed of my disrespectful reaction to his authority. My brothers had already defied him – shamed him – by leaving, and now here I was, telling him that I was planning to do the exact same thing. The third one to go in such a short space of time. It affected him deeply. He didn't want to be the one whose children needed to be prayed for by the other cult members. He hated that I was rebelling against him and against the way I had been brought up. He was so committed to the cult, I doubt he could understand why I so desperately wanted to be away from it. He didn't see the world the same way I did, that much was clear: he saw no need to leave, no need to experience new things and a new way of living. He had everything he wanted right where he wanted it, and, for him, the rest of the world was nothing more than an abstract irritation. There was no way he could ever have empathized with the way I – and my brothers – were feeling.

I think he was also terrified about what people would think of the family – what they would think of him – when they found out what was going on. The other members of the cult would know that he had 'worldly, disobedient' children. They would have to pray for us. I imagine that it was one of the worst things that could happen to my father, being the man that he was. It went against everything he had tried to build for himself, and he couldn't handle it. The thought of being looked down on, of being pitied by his fellow community members, was just too much.

He finally calmed down enough for me to inform him that I'd already given the owner of the construction company my two weeks' notice, that it was too late to do anything about it now and that I definitely wasn't going to change my mind. I held my ground, determined not to show him how nervous I felt about telling him the news. He went ice cold. He told me curtly that I needed to go to the church, that I had to go and find my employer and tell him I'd changed my mind. He said that I had to apologize to him and then go straight back to work, as though the whole drama had never happened. Out of sight, out of mind. I was supposed to put the whole thing behind me and get on with the life I had been living since I was a child. As if it was that easy to forget about all of my concerns, about all of my hopes for getting out and all of my dreams for a cult-free future. He just didn't understand. I didn't expect him to.

Well, forgetting wasn't an option. I felt sorry for my dad, really I did. His whole life had been built around this image of how things were supposed to be and I don't think he could really see how fragile it all was, how brittle was the façade that was holding us all together. I think it must have been a shock for him to find out how my brothers and I really felt about it all; it wasn't like we'd ever been able to speak to him about it. He'd never given us the opportunity. I don't know; maybe he really believed that staying in the cult was the right thing to do, that our way of life had depth. Maybe he really thought that he was doing the very best he could for his family, and was concerned about what would happen to us for going against his efforts. He was certainly a man of conviction, I can say that about him for sure.

I just don't think he really got the irony of working so hard to keep up appearances when, clearly, there was so much going on underneath that was never spoken of, so much that was being hidden away from everyone else. He had to keep up his image of being a success, and that obviously meant leaving out certain family secrets which would embarrass him and question his position as head of the household. The actions of my brothers and I had clearly put a dent in that. I don't feel bad about it – he needed to be shown what his actions had done to the family – except for the fact of what it did to my mother.

I knew that leaving the cult would mean leaving my parents. While I could make my peace with leaving my father – after all, he was part of the reason I wanted to go – leaving my mother really hurt. I knew it would. She worked so hard for all of us, for very little thanks, and I felt very guilty for leaving her behind. I loved her, and I never doubted that she loved me. She was a big part of the reason I didn't leave sooner.

I knew, however, that I had to go. I had been born into that life, I hadn't chosen it for myself, and I wanted to build my own life, one that I *had* chosen for myself. I had to make the break then or else I never would, and I don't even want to consider what would have happened had that been the case. It doesn't bear thinking about.

ELLE BENÉT

So I summoned up all of the courage I held within me and I told my father that I wouldn't go to the church, I wouldn't find my employer, and I wouldn't apologize to him for my decision. Even though it was hard, I made sure I stood my ground. It was the only way to make myself heard and understood. I told my father that I wasn't going to go back to my job. I told him that if it mattered so much to him, then *he* could apologize to the owner of the construction firm. He could make amends if he really wanted to. He was the one who was clearly upset by the whole thing. If he wanted to apologize, then he could, but I certainly wasn't going to, no matter what he said or how he tried to convince me.

Thinking back on it now, I'm certain that my mother was worried I was going to be beaten for being a 'rebel'. Though he never physically harmed my mother or me at any point in our lives, it didn't ease her apprehension in that moment. She must have been so scared, standing there, listening to us yelling and arguing. I can only imagine that the sudden eruption of conflict – of a lifetime's worth of resentments that had been slowly building up and of frustrations that had been kept under the surface for so long, suddenly breaking out into the open – must have been shocking to behold. I think she understood, though – at least on some level – that I had reached the point when I wasn't going to put up with it anymore. I think she sort of understood that I was more than ready for a physical confrontation with my father, if that's what it was going to take.

I was certainly ready for it. I had all these years of anger built up in me. The anger came from so many places that I hardly knew where to focus it. There was the obvious anger at being forced to live my life conforming to someone else's beliefs. The anger at never having been appreciated, despite how much my life was affected by the beliefs of the cult. The anger at what had happened to my brothers, and how my father never realized that it wasn't normal to hurt your children like he did. I was also angry at the confusion I felt: I was confused by how I had been made to live, and by what I really thought about the world. I had to question my whole life, and I felt that my entire existence had been built on a lie. I value honesty above almost all else; the thought that my entire life was based on foundations that were shaky at best and downright falsehoods at worst really made the anger start to roil and take shape. It had been building up inside me for a while, and it was only a matter of time before I was forced to address it. Address it, accept it, and make the best decision I could: to leave.

A particular situation comes to mind that stirs the fire in my belly even now:

"Mom, what's going to happen to those people who don't go to our church?"

ELLE BENÉT

My mother thinks about this for a minute. "If they don't repent and go to church, they won't make it to Heaven."

I'm quiet as I take all of this in. I'm only eight years old, and it's quite a big idea to digest at this stage in my life. I have been brought up to believe that if you live a good life, Heaven is the reward you are given. The thought that people who don't go to our church are unlikely to make it there shocks me deeply.

The family is on the way to a church service. My parents, brothers and I pile into the car to make the trip. I sit quietly in the back seat, thinking about what my mother has told me. I press my nose against the window, looking out at the other children as we make our way to the church.

These are the children my mother says will not make it to Heaven. They're not going to Heaven and yet... they look so happy. I don't understand it. What have they done that means they could be deserving of the punishment of being kept out of Heaven?

I wonder whether the truth is that I am very lucky. I have been born into a family that just so happens to go to the one church that is going to be saved, the only church of believers that will make it into Heaven. What is the likelihood of that? My mom said that people have to repent and start going to church if they want to be saved. My eight-year-old self wonders how everyone will fit into our church: it's only small. This worries me greatly.

There is so much, even in that one small incident, that makes me angry. Only the members of our church would go to Heaven, apparently – people had to join and repent if they wanted to go, and yet the cult was not welcoming to outsiders who wanted to join us, how could that even be possible? I was so tired of all the contradictions. How could it be so exclusive and shut out so many people? Even to my eight-year-old brain, it all seemed so wrong: my perspective of the cult began to change then, even if I didn't realize it at the time. I was starting to distinguish between right and wrong, independent of my father's thinking and the way I'd been brought up, and the more I began to see – with the beatings at home and the way the cult treated outsiders – the more it became apparent that something was terribly wrong with the way I'd been taught to act, to live, to *be*. Was the way I was being brought up wrong? Why was everything – the religious part of the cult, in particular – so confusing? Nothing seemed to make sense to me, and I was starting to wonder if my entire life was, in fact, being built upon a huge, devastating lie.

By the time I reached adulthood, there was so much more that seemed completely wrong – that actually *was* wrong – that it was inevitable that it would all come pouring out at some point. And come pouring out, it certainly did.

The anger had been bubbling away for so long, trapped down inside of me while I fought hard to contain it, to keep it locked away as I had been brought up to do. The thing is, I think anger is like a volcano: you can fill yourself with it for years, but eventually it will make you feel incredibly bloated and it will end up simply bursting out of you. It's highly dangerous and completely inevitable. There's only so much pressure you can take until, finally, you have to let it out like lava spewing from the side of a previously innocuous-looking mountain. The pressure blows you apart in the end if you don't do anything about it, if you don't do something to relieve it, and – ultimately – deal with it.

There's a lesson in there, I'm sure. A lesson that says there's only so much you can deal with on your own, that even if you are the most independent-minded person in the world, you still need a support network of some kind: you need people to be there for you. Even if you don't need or want them to do anything in particular, just having them there can be enough. It lets you know that you're not alone; that if you need help, you can find it. Keeping all that hurt and anger locked up inside you isn't healthy, either for you or for the focus of all that feeling. It helps to spread the load a little. That's partly why I'm writing this; I feel like in letting this out, it's some sort of therapy. It's cathartic. And I hope it will inspire anyone reading it to think about the people in their lives who would be there for them, no matter what, to think that no matter how hopeless things can sometimes seem, there is always something better waiting for you. You just have to go out and find it for yourself.

We're so different – my father and I. For him, it was normal to let his anger show and to take out his frustrations on the people around him. I'm the complete opposite. I like to keep everything inside so that when I do let my emotions show, people know that I'm serious. I like to think that I can carry on, no matter how much I have to deal with – until, of course, there comes a point when I just have to let it all out. *Somehow*. Maybe it was his exuberance that made me like that, I don't know. All I know is that no matter how closely related you are to someone, it doesn't necessarily mean that you are in any way compatible. Despite the good relationships I had with my brothers and the love I felt for my mother, I came to understand that flesh and blood are not always the ties that bind. Realizing and accepting this made me feel much better about the decision I had made: my father and I were simply too different to be able to tolerate each other any longer.

After that confrontation with my father, I soon began taking refuge at my brothers' house, sleeping over there and taking some comfort in them and their new surroundings. While very basic, the fact that their home was away from my parents was all I really needed. The whole place was covered in a dark blue carpet which didn't look like it had been cleaned properly for years, and because of this, you never wanted to take your shoes off. There was very little lighting, and this – merged with the dark, dirty carpet – made the place seem dim and dull. There was very little furniture; just a couch to sit on – no table and chairs, no place to sit and eat a meal. The kitchen was tiny and there was no backyard. It was the complete opposite of the house we had grown up in, but I felt safer there than I ever did at home. It was a place that was free of the stresses and hurts we had grown up with; a little sanctuary that my brothers had created for themselves, and one that I was lucky to be able to share with them. I felt as though I could breathe properly there, and it allowed me to imagine the possibility of a new life more vividly than ever before. It was no longer an abstract dream. Their place was the kind of environment (although not physically) that I strive to provide for my children now: a safe, loving, worry free house that was a home, not a prison.

Not long after, the day I would finally and irrevocably leave the cult arrived. It was an extremely important day: it was the point when I stopped living someone else's life and started living my own. Leaving proved to be more of a mental challenge than a physical one. The physical aspect of it was actually fairly easy: I simply walked out of the house. Yet with so many emotions flying around – as well as the almost overwhelming fear of the unknown – it took quite a bit of willpower to leave. I would have to learn how to live an entirely different life, and the scale of the task seemed huge; it was completely daunting to someone who had led a relatively sheltered life until then. But I was curious about this other world and what it held – I wanted to explore it and discover everything for myself. That curiosity was stronger than the fear of the unknown, and it helped me to make the break I so desperately needed. Curiosity is important; we can achieve so much simply through our desire to know more, to do more, to see more. So even though leaving was difficult for me, it was something I simply had to do.

I prefer to think of my leaving and everything that happened after as positive, good things that got me to where I am today. After all, we are constantly moving forwards, and ever since the day I left the cult – despite the stress and anxiety I felt about the big, wide, world – I've been moving on with my life. By moving forward one step at a time, by putting one foot in front of the other, I have been travelling away from my old life and towards a new one filled with potential. Every single footstep has taken me on the exciting, scary, exploratory path that has brought me to my destination today.

Leaving was a self-preservation thing. I had to do it, and I had to do it right then.

ELLE BENÉT

From then on, I knew that unless I reverted to their religious beliefs, I couldn't associate with my parents again. It was against the practices of the cult; the members had to keep themselves separate from outsiders. I was familiar with this thinking – all those years of being skeptical of newcomers and not being permitted to associate with the worldly children had taught me all too well that once I left, that would be that. The rules that had for so long kept me within the confines of the cult would now keep me out of it. The thought, while scary, was also freeing in its own way.

Mostly, though, I had a strange feeling of emptiness about the whole thing; I knew that I had severed my connections with my parents and yet they were still there, only a few minutes away from where I was living, alive and well. They were always there on the periphery – there and yet not there. It's a hard emotional journey to go through, but I suppose we all do it in some guise or other. We all leave home at some point and set up on our own, away from how and where we grew up. Everything might have been heightened in the cult, but the fundamentals were largely the same. The main difference was that after I left, there was no going back.

And yet it would have been so easy to go back. On my very worst days, setting up in my new life, I could just about understand why others who had left had eventually decided to go back to what they knew. To what was familiar. It would have been so much simpler to just give in and go back to the relative security and regimented structure of cult life, but I never wanted my struggle to be for nothing, especially after the whole showdown with my father. I wanted to prove that I could be my own person and make my own existence without giving in to help from back home. I had been struggling for so many years: what would have been the point of admitting defeat as soon as I had got what I wanted, just because it was sometimes difficult, sometimes a little scary? Life is always going to have its challenges, even in ideal circumstances. No matter what happened, I had to keep trying. Giving up just wasn't an option for me.

The neighborhood my brothers and I lived in was a place where – how should I put this? – it was advisable to stay indoors at night. It was all we could afford and we all made a pact that however bad things were for us, we would never go back to the cult. We would much prefer to sleep outside in the cold rather than go back there. We were united in our aims, and that helped me greatly; we may not have had much, but we had a roof over our heads and, most importantly, we had each other. We weren't going through it all alone.

In the back of my mind, however, I could never quite shake the thought that what we had created together as a small family unit wasn't going to last forever. We were all young. We all had our own, individual lives ahead of us. For now, we were on the same path, taking comfort in each other and depending on each other to make our new lives work out, but it was only a matter of time before something shifted and our lives would be forever altered. I was always aware of how fragile the state of things was and yet I couldn't quite embrace that fact, either. I needed my brothers: they were my support, my family, and I wasn't ready to let them go just yet.

For the time being, we were all in it together. We shared in the pain and the difficulties and the satisfaction of our achievements. We were all working, yet money was tight and there never seemed to be enough to go around.

One of my brothers and I were both still working as personal trainers at the same gym, and the nature of the job meant that our funds were unpredictable from week to week. We had to find our own clients and some weeks were definitely leaner than others. Another main problem we had was that it was always hard to gauge exactly how much we were going to bring home, so we couldn't plan or budget our money like many others do. The added challenge was the newness of it all; this was my first real job outside of the community I had grown up in, and for quite a while I found it hard to get clients. Having never had the chance to talk or interact with outsiders in any way, I was quite reserved in my nature and unsure of how to go about approaching people. My lack of confidence in this respect hindered my ability to make friends with new people, and it was a real struggle to try and convince clients to choose me as their trainer. The whole thing was far tougher than I had expected, and it highlighted just how different I was from others my age, simply because of my upbringing and the rules I'd had to adhere to during that time.

Adjusting to my new life was difficult; I'd come from a safe, structured community where you could trust everyone as you knew that their intentions were good. We didn't have to fear anyone within the cult, we knew that we could go and talk to other members without anything bad happening. I soon learned that you couldn't think this way out in the 'real world'. Not everyone was nice, not everyone was on your side, not everyone would appreciate you approaching them. I had to realize – fast – that not everyone could be trusted. There were bad people in this world who did bad things, and crime was something you simply had to be aware of. There were other things to get used to after leaving the cult, too; simple things such as being able to wear what I wanted and to be able to live my life without having to plan it around all the religious services I was used to. This thought of being 'free' should have been an exciting concept to me, but – at the time – I had other, more important things to worry about. I was in pure survival mode, more concerned with getting food to eat and money to pay the bills with rather than the fact that I could now wear pants and make up. I simply didn't have the time to think about these little things; I had to put everything I had into staying alive.

Meanwhile, my eldest brother was working in another state. We managed – just – but it definitely wasn't easy. My brothers took on most of the responsibility for paying the bills with their wages, and I contributed by pulling in enough money to put gas in the tank of our car with some left over so we could buy food and clothing, but there were times when our budget didn't stretch as far as we needed it to go. It was something we were completely unaccustomed to, and getting used to the new way of living took some work. We'd gone from the relative safety of the cult (at least in terms of relying on our parents and not having to fend for ourselves), to this large, seemingly endless world where we had no one to rely on but each other. It's not an exaggeration to say that it was an extremely overwhelming time for me.

Fending for yourself is scary, especially when there isn't much money and you're always wondering whether or not you'll be able to eat from one day to the next. I didn't feel like I could ask my brothers for help, either: they had already done so much for me – and they were struggling, too. I never wanted them to feel guilty because they couldn't help me, or to ask them for food when they already had so little for themselves. I didn't want them to go without because of me. They had, after all, left the cult of their own accord. I had simply followed.

The irony was that there were two fully stocked fridges less than fifteen minutes away from where we were staying, both of them packed full with goodies and all the food you could ever want – the only problem being that they were at our parents' house. That was one thing we always had to be grateful for when growing up in the community: it might not necessarily have been the 'normal', loving upbringing we had wanted, but there had always been plenty of food to eat. We had never had to worry about any of our basic needs – money and shelter and sustenance. We had that much security, at least.

And isn't it weird, the way an area can change so much in such a short distance? On my parents' side of the neighborhood was all the affluence you could imagine. The people had plenty of money, and in terms of both needs and luxuries, they wanted for nothing. A couple of miles away, where my brothers and I were living, it was a very different story. People really struggled. We were living a hand-to-mouth existence and – while I feel that ultimately I am a stronger person because of it and the experience taught me a lot about personal endurance as well as how difficult things are for so many people – that didn't stop the injustice of it all from stinging.

My pride and my dignity wouldn't let me go back to my mother and ask her for food and other necessities. Those two things were the pillars of my new life; even when I had nothing else, I had them. I knew that I couldn't compromise them. They were worth more than money, more than the certainty of regular meals, more than my old life.

To an outsider, it must have looked so weird. I'm sure people must have wondered why I didn't just go back and ask my parents for help. It wasn't as though they didn't have the resources, and it would have been the most sensible thing to do, I'm sure. It would have been what many other people would have done, people who didn't grow up in the environment that my brothers and I did. Yet to do that would have been admitting failure. Plus, I didn't want to give any false hope to my mother that we may be returning. It would have been cruel to give her hope like that only to leave again once we had got what we needed. So, despite the emotional and physical pain of it all, we made the decision together and chose to stay away from our old house.

Have you ever been hungry? Not just a little bit hungry, not just hungry with an empty stomach in the way that often happens when you've not eaten all day yet dinner is still hours away. Not like that, but really, properly hungry to the point where your body hurts? It's hard to think about anything else. It's not because of greed; it's basic human nature. You need food to survive, so if you deprive your body of it –willingly or not – then your body starts to protest. It sends you all the signals it can to tell you that it's empty and it needs more fuel. It won't let you forget it. It weakens your body, and constantly nags away at not only your stomach, but your brain, too. It gives you all of these physical signs that you need to eat, and then – because we are sentient creatures – it tortures you some more because your mind just can't let it go, you can't stop thinking about it, about how hungry you are and just how much you want to – *need* to – eat. It becomes completely overwhelming. It's hard to think clearly about anything other than food: getting it and eating it as fast as you possibly can is the only thing you can concern yourself with. You start to imagine an abundance of food, how amazing it would be to have just a single taste of your favorite dish. Or even your least favorite dish. Anything. It makes life seem very simple and it gets your priorities straight in a hurry. It's a necessity: you've got to eat, not being able to is just horrible.

Couple that with an emotional hunger, a desire for love and comfort and just a little bit of normalcy that you find conspicuously lacking in your life and you have yourself quite a potent cocktail. It's hard to admit that you're not managing as well on your own as you would want to be. It's harder to know what to do when there is literally nowhere to turn and no one to depend on but yourself.

Sometimes, it would've been nice to just have someone there to look after me, someone there to help me fix my problems and offer solutions when I couldn't think of any on my own. I think sometimes that it's a miracle I kept my sanity intact. Then I remember that I had so much drive, so much purpose, that I probably could have withstood practically anything, as long as there was always that sense that I could make it in the end. As long as there was always hope.

That's the essence of the American Dream right there, and the dreams of so many others around the world; people who fight every day – against all odds – in the hope that tomorrow will be just a little bit better than today. It's not about massive wealth and other riches and consumption to excess; it's about being steady, having focus, working hard and never, ever giving up. And, if you're lucky, you just might succeed. Tomorrow might be that tiny bit better than today and you'll never know pride like it. Believe me.

That was how I got through. Even in those darkest times, when I was sleeping on the floor, freezing cold because we couldn't afford any heating, and close to starving because we couldn't afford any food, it got me through. There's always tomorrow. Always. You pick yourself up and you start again.

***THEY* MADE ME DO IT**

It's funny really, how you often don't notice just how much a person does for you until they are suddenly no longer there to do it – the phrase 'you don't know what you've got 'till it's gone' comes to mind. That was how I felt about my mother after I left home. I missed her, not just everything that she used to do for me and the rest of the family, but *her*. Her value as a person and the companionship that we used to share. I missed everything about her. I loved her and I guess I was still just a little girl inside, wanting my mommy to come and make it all better for me. Suddenly, I was in a situation where I had no one to depend on but myself and I felt her absence keenly.

I missed her so much that one day I finally gave in and went home to visit her. I chose to go on Thanksgiving. After all, I thought, if you can't visit your family on Thanksgiving, then when can you? It would also be a chance to see my two other brothers who had chosen to stay behind in the cult when the rest of us had left for our new neighborhood. It had been a long time since I'd spent any time with them, and I eagerly anticipated seeing them all again, despite the trepidation I felt about going back there.

The look on my mother's face when I showed up was enough to say it all: it let me know that she really did love me, despite everything – despite all the hard times and the tension that had existed between us from time to time. She loved me. I had never really doubted that fact, but it was wonderful to have it verified and to see her so happy to see me.

I love moments like that. Those times when people are unguarded, caught unaware, and they just can't help the way they react. Sometimes, with some people, it's the only time you ever see their genuine feelings or emotions – that split second when they look up and you see what they're really thinking, before their mask goes back on and the moment is lost forever. It's reassuring, somehow. It lets you know that, really, we all have a public face to mask the one we wear in private and that it's okay to do that because everyone else does it, too. Everyone has a hidden life inside of themselves that only rarely breaks through to be glimpsed on the surface. We all have our own personal icebergs. We all spend so much time pretending, to protect ourselves and each other. Those brief moments when the façade drops are so precious. I'll never forget it.

My father, on the other hand, didn't seem to express the same exuberance that my mother was outwardly portraying. If he was happy to see me at all, he didn't show it; his expression was somber, guarded. He just looked at me – long and hard – and said that if I wanted to stay, I had to take out my earrings.

THEY MADE ME DO IT

As I've mentioned, earrings were not permitted in the cult: jewelry was seen as gaudy and frivolous. It seems to me that that's why most people like it, yet naturally, in the backwards world of the cult, that was the reason it was so loathed. Jewelry is such a personal thing. It reflects your tastes and style and preferences, and that level of individuality was feared by the members of the community I'd grown up in. It was something to be suppressed, not encouraged. Expressing yourself through your appearance was simply not allowed.

Being able to wear earrings and other jewelry – having the ability to choose for myself how I wanted to dress – were now important things that allowed me to distinguish myself from how I had once lived. I knew the real reason why my father didn't like my earrings: they were a sure sign that I didn't belong in the cult anymore.

Of course, the sensible thing to do would have been to just agree. In the grand scheme of things, the jewelry I wear in my ears is a minor detail, despite its significance for me. I should probably have taken out my earrings and stayed for dinner, as had been my intention in the first place.

But when it came to it, I simply couldn't do it. I had made a promise to myself that I would never be beholden to my father again and that I would never put his wishes above mine. I wasn't about to start following his orders again. So I kept in my earrings and – despite the fact I knew without doubt that my mother wanted me to just give in and comply – I left. I was an adult with the ability to make my own decisions, so I made one. It hurt to walk away from my mother like that – again – but I think that it is *so* important to never compromise your values, or else there is no point in having them in the first place. I made a choice based on what I believed, which, in a weird way, is sort of what my parents had always raised me to do. Believe.

It just so happened that what I believed in was different than what they had hoped.

I'm fairly certain that my mother never told my father, but sometimes she would call me to say hi. I think she felt a little bit lost in the house without me and my brothers there; she had spent so many years looking after us, making us the center of her world, that she must have been at a loss when we all started to leave the house, one by one. I hope it provided some sort of comfort to her, to be able to call and talk to me. I just wish she would have talked about subjects of actual substance. I had hoped that those phone calls might offer us a small way in which we could reconnect and get to know each other in a new capacity, but it didn't work out as I might've hoped.

All my life, all I ever wanted was for her to be there and to give me advice in the way that other mothers do for their daughters, but any attempt I made at 'proper' conversation would be shut down and replaced with something else. I remember once, I asked her for some advice because I genuinely wanted to know what she would do. Her response was: "think about what God would do."

I can understand why she would always draw things back round to God: she had spent so long in the cult that it had become a comfort to her – that way of life and the order which it laid down for her to follow. She might well have been craving to talk to me properly, but it was as though she would be losing something of herself if she did. So everything was about God instead, as though she was afraid to offer answers on her own, as though her opinions were secondary to those of God and the cult.

I wanted to tell her that maybe, just maybe, talking about other things might help her find herself instead. It might help her make sense of things if she let herself explore them, if she opened her mind up to new ideas and her own opinions. I wanted to tell her that faith isn't meant to be restrictive: at its most beautiful, it can be immensely freeing. Liberating. A very personal thing, not something that you're forced to live with. Unfortunately, that freedom of belief is something that gets lost far too easily.

ELLE BENÉT

As I had predicted, my newfound life didn't last long in its original incarnation. My brothers and I lived together for about a year in total before everything changed again and I once more found myself in need of a new solution.

It was a strange time. On one level, I was worried for myself and what I was going to do, and yet on another level I was unspeakably proud and happy for both of my brothers. You see, my eldest brother had applied for a position in DC and had been successful in getting the job. My other brother was planning to move in with his girlfriend. They had both worked hard and were finally getting what they wanted – what they deserved. I was thrilled for them, but I couldn't help feeling as though I had been left behind. I had left the cult, but my new life had yet to really get off the ground, to become what I'd always dreamed about. What had been exciting and overwhelming at first was turning into something much more concerning. It was a low time for me.

I felt like I was being shoved behind the wheel of a car for the first time, right in the middle of rush hour, and being told to drive myself home. I didn't know how to operate the controls of the life I was living. I wasn't even sure where 'home' was, or where it was I was meant to be heading towards. I was worried about where I was going to go and what I was going to do and I felt I couldn't afford to live on my own. All I knew was that I was hurtling along at full speed and I couldn't find the brakes.

I got depressed a lot during that time. In so many ways, I was so self-sufficient. I was independent and I knew better than most people of the same age how to look after myself and deal with things alone. Then, in other ways, I craved human contact. I could look after myself but I still wanted people there. I never wanted to be dependent on anyone, but when I made that choice, I never wanted to be completely on my own, either. Suddenly the scales were tipping too much towards the side of 'alone' rather than 'independent' and, while they were still swinging and failing to settle, things seemed fairly scary.

Despite all of this, the whole thing turned out to be an immensely positive experience. You never know how much you can achieve until you have to, and you never know how strong you are until you have no choice but to be strong. You just have to believe that you will find a solution and that you have the capability to do whatever it is you need to do. You'll find a way. Of course, it's easy to say this with the benefit of hindsight; while you're in that moment, it can be hard to fathom ever coming out the other side. But believe me, you will. I did.

I started to properly pick myself up when I – quite by chance – ran into my cousin in the gym where I worked.

I hadn't seen her for years but I recognized her instantly. She had lived in the cult, too, and we had grown up in the same community, although she had left years before I had, and the fact that she was about ten years older than me meant I didn't really know her too well.

Still, there were very few people who really understood my situation and what it was like, so I felt an intense kinship with her. After all, she had lived it, too. She knew all about it and had had many of the same experiences that I'd had. I went over to her in the gym that day and we started talking. From then on, I saw her more and more regularly. I told her all about my brothers, about how thrilled I was for them and yet how desperate I felt about them leaving, and how I didn't know what I was going to do next.

It must have been kismet. One day after meeting up with her, she called me and asked if I would like to go and live with her and her friend. I accepted, obviously. I was still distraught over the thought of my beloved brothers leaving, but her invitation made me feel like there was a next step and that I was strong enough to take it. She gave me the soft landing I so badly needed at that time in my life and I will always be so grateful to her and her friend for making a place for me in their home and in their lives.

All too soon, the day arrived when my eldest brother was due to leave for DC. I went out for a walk in order to avoid having to watch him pack. I just needed to put it out of my mind for a little bit longer, to spend just a few more moments imagining that this was another ordinary day, and that everything would stay exactly the same as it had been since we'd left the cult. I went back to watch him leave, though. I really wanted to hug him goodbye but I just couldn't bring myself to do it. I knew that if I did, I would cry and I didn't want him to see that; I needed him to know that I would be okay without him. He didn't need the burden of my tears on his conscience when he had done so well for himself and was off to take the next amazing step on his journey. I had my own journey to travel, my own path, and although I was devastated to see my brother leave, I knew that I had to let him continue with his, walking on towards his own destination.

So instead of hugging him I crossed my arms, as though it would somehow bar the tears that were undoubtedly beginning to well, from flowing. And it worked, too… or at least it did until he pulled off the driveway. As soon as his little car disappeared from my view, I uncrossed my arms as, simultaneously, the tears began to flow freely.

For a brief moment, I felt like everything was crumbling around me, simply because I had decided to leave the cult. Everything had happened because of that one decision and, as a result, my life had collapsed in on itself. I felt like I was being punished.

ELLE BENÉT

I will never forget that day – it's as vivid now as it was back then. I think it was only my cousin's phone call and her offer for me to live with her that kept me going after that. Without my brothers, I was completely bereft.

As time passes and the night grows deeper, old pictures fill my mind. I can still see all those things that affected me so much when I was younger: my brother leaving for DC, the look of astonishing love in my mother's eyes, the lack of love in my father's... I can see it all and I can see now how all of those moments, all of the ways in which they played a part in my life, have affected me and made me the person I am today. They are the reason I'm here right now.

I know I should be sleeping, but I know that if I try, sleep won't come. Somewhere, a clock is ticking. I listen to it for a minute before turning back to the task at hand.

THEY MADE ME DO IT

WHEN LIFE GIVES YOU LEMONS…

One of the most negative aspects about this period of my life was being destitute when I moved out of my parents' home. It can be immensely soul destroying to work so hard to make a life for yourself, and to still find yourself with so little to show for it. My brothers and I worked as much as we possibly could, yet often we failed to bring food home at the end of the day. Being hungry has to be one of the worst experiences of my life. It makes you desperate in a way you can never know unless you have been there yourself. It makes your whole life revolve around something that you used to take for granted. It was something I couldn't have foreseen and it definitely wasn't anything I could have prepared myself for; while there were many things wrong with living in the cult community, I'd never gone without food before.

So many people live like that, then and now; so many people are hungry, in this country and many others. So many of those people live so close to wealth and plenty, as my brothers and I did, and yet they go without. They hurt and their thoughts are consumed with where the next meal is going to come from, an issue plenty of other people never have to think twice about. I never did before I moved away from home.

It was one of the hardest things I have ever gone through, but all the same, I am grateful that I *did* go through it; it makes me feel genuine gratitude for the things that I have now, no matter how small they are. All of those things that we call 'basic needs' – the need for shelter, for food, and for clothing – are more precious than we know. If you have a roof over your head, clothes on your back and food to eat, take a moment to think how truly wonderful that really is.

The whole thing has made me much more compassionate to people who don't have these things. I've lived the life they live, and I know how hard it is. The vast majority of them are simply trying to get through life as best they can. I think that's something we can all appreciate and empathize with. Gratitude for food and the other simple needs that I now have in my life has changed the way I think about everything. It was a hard lesson to learn, but I'm glad now that I *did* learn it.

Hunger made me weak then, but the experience has made me stronger now. If I hadn't gone through that hardship – that time of being so completely empty – my life wouldn't be so full of great things today.

The other negative aspect of this time in my life that I was really affected by was the abrupt transition into an entirely different world, a world of which I had very little knowledge and practically no experience. Even the things that most people find easy – going up and introducing myself to people, something that my job depended on – I found very difficult. I didn't have the same social skills and tools as everyone else, and it took a while to learn how to adapt to my new job and my new life. This was both daunting and frustrating; I found it hard to relate to people, and I didn't know how to get them on my side, such as when I was trying to persuade gym members to be my clients. This made life complicated not only at work but also when trying to make new friends or simply talking to people when I was out and about. I just wasn't used to it.

I had never really felt as though I was part of the cult, and for a while I didn't really feel like I was part of the wider world, either. It was as if I was drifting, not really fitting in anywhere. My saving grace was the fact that I was so determined to make it work: I was sure that I had made the right decision, that my situation would improve and that I would become an active, productive, happy member of society. I kept that in mind as I learned how to interact with the world at large, and I never lost sight of my goal. This practice at striving for a particular target has helped me ever since: now, if I want something, I just go for it, and I don't let anything get in the way of achieving my aim.

That self-belief was hugely valuable to me. It helped to teach me independence. It taught me how to live away from what I had previously known, and how to fit into a strange new environment where I hardly knew anyone and had to make it on my own steam, or else fail. I learned how to deal with everything that life could think to throw at me, how to stay standing even when I felt like my world was being ripped apart and – thanks to my cousin's wonderful offer – how to know when to accept a kind and helping hand.

CHAPTER THREE

By the time my brothers had moved out of the house, it was 2005. It feels like a lifetime ago; so much has happened between then and now. Between 2005 and 2007, I was completely focused on sorting myself out. I knew three important things: that I didn't want to go back to the cult; that I needed to find a new direction for my life; and that I wanted to see my brothers more. Armed with nothing but that knowledge, I set about trying to achieve my goals.

For much of that period, I was very busy and productive, and I filled my days well enough. But not that much really stands out when I think of those years. I suppose it's a bit like when you look back on your school years: you know you've spent all this time in education and you know it's been worth it and that you ultimately got a lot out of it, but there are very few distinct, truly memorable things about that period of your life. Of course, you know whether you enjoyed it or hated it, whether you were popular or not, whether you did well or not. But I'd bet good money that most people can't remember all that much about school, at least not when considering how much time they spent there. That time in my life was a little like that… important yet transitory.

Moving in with my cousins was the first time I had lived solely with other women and, after the repressive nature of the cult and the protectiveness I felt towards my brothers when I lived with them, it was liberating. I was grateful for both of them and I really valued their friendship and the space they had made for me in their lives. The support they offered me in this world I was still learning was of a different kind to anything I had known before. I guess women just think slightly differently and I believe that they helped to shape my thinking, too. After so many years living mainly with men – where the man was the head of the household and the views of others weren't exactly given much merit – the experience of living with the two women has definitely shaped me for the better. My time spent with them was invaluable.

One thing I recall clearly is that my time was consumed with working and saving money – I was completely determined to be able to buy my own place. That was one thing that would signal I had truly made it away from the cult: a home that I could call my own, that would always be there at the end of the day. My own space to use how I wanted, without any interference from anyone else. My living situation was the biggest issue on my mind: I knew it was still so unstable and that I might have to move on again at any time, despite the support I received from my new roommates. I didn't want anywhere big or flashy, but more than ever before, I was desperate to have somewhere I could call my own. I felt like then, I would be able to say that I had achieved my dreams. I would be a success. I would be able to admit that leaving the cult had been the right thing to do, the best possible thing I could have done at that time in my life. I already knew that, of course, but I wanted confirmation. A solid, tangible result, something I could touch and see for myself. Something real.

It seems to be a common thing: people often remark that they don't really feel like they're properly grown up until they have somewhere of their own, that they bought with their hard-earned money and that they continue to work hard to keep. Something for themselves, something that they truly deserve. I just wish it wasn't so hard to achieve that dream; I didn't know it at the time, but it was a theme that would raise its head again later in my life. It's difficult to comprehend just how fragile life is, until your livelihood is under threat of being taken away. That's how I felt then – that the foundations I had been painstakingly constructing for the past couple of years might crumble without warning – and, in a different way, it's how I feel now. But that's another story, one I'll come to in due course.

I managed to achieve what I set out to do, though. The goal of owning my own home gave me a renewed focus like never before: suddenly I had something tangible and definable that I knew I wanted to achieve, and I put all of my resources into it. I worked hard for a year, scrimped and saved wherever I could, appreciated the unwavering support of my cousin and then, finally, I had enough money to put a deposit on a tiny studio apartment. It was such a rewarding experience and a huge relief.

All the time, my brothers were still very much on my mind. I wanted more than anything for us to get back together and I felt as though, if I managed to better myself, then it might just happen. By the time I moved into my little studio, the eldest was still in DC while the other had relocated to Florida. They were achieving their goals and I thought that if I could do the same, then at the very least, we would be on a level playing field and I would be able to see them more. We might not be together in the way that we were after we left our parents' house, but we would still be bonded by all we had done afterwards. We would be equals. I wouldn't feel like I was running to catch up with them anymore.

The studio I lived in wasn't much, but it was mine. It was small (about 350 square feet) and I didn't even have enough money to buy furniture, so I slept on the floor instead of in a bed. It was bare and basic, the lack of furnishings and wall-to-wall white carpeting making it seem even blander. Everything about the place was tiny: tiny hallway, tiny kitchen area, tiny closet, tiny bathroom. It had one window, but it only looked out over the parking lot. The studio was also about fifteen minutes away from my parents' neighborhood and beautiful house, but I felt like I was living a whole world away. It was just such a completely different existence.

However, it was all a small price to pay to have somewhere of my very own. I used to lie there with nothing but a sheet over me, using my clothes as a pillow, eyes closed but still wide awake, my mind buzzing. It is always easier to think at night, when there are fewer demands on my time and fewer distractions; all I would want would be to sleep, but my mind would keep on turning in the dark. I couldn't stop it anymore than I could afford my own furniture.

Sometimes, I used to think about my parents. It is inevitable that no matter how much time has passed since I left them, my mother and father will always have a place in my mind and my memories. That will never change, no matter how many years have gone by. During the time in my studio, I would think about how they were only fifteen minutes away, so close I could almost reach out and touch them. I used to imagine my mother, lying in her bed, staring up at the ceiling while I lay on my floor, staring up at a ceiling that was the same but different. We were so close and yet so, so far apart. I wondered if she used to lie in her bed and think about her daughter. I hope she thought good things about me.

THEY MADE ME DO IT

I knew that living in the studio would be a temporary thing. It had to be, really. My dreams were much bigger than where I was currently living, but that didn't stop me from being proud of myself all the same. It was an important stepping stone on my journey, a vital footprint that I was leaving behind before carrying on to something bigger. I also knew that if I was going to do something with those bigger dreams, I would have to be bolder.

It's so easy to play it safe. People do it all the time. I have known so many people who grew up with amazing dreams and yet have settled for something less than they were made for. "That's life," seems to be a common explanation for the trend. "Things happen, dreams don't always work out, you don't always get what you want."

That's certainly true enough, but I knew even then that if I was going to fail to achieve my dreams, then it wasn't going to be because I didn't try hard enough. Playing it safe was not an option for me. If I wanted to play it safe, I never would have left the cult in the first place. I have to believe that you get what you work for: if you put the effort in, you will be rewarded in return – even if the rewards don't necessarily come straight away. I had a goal, and I was going to reach it, no matter what.

So I pushed myself. It would have been easier, I'm sure, to stay where I was, living in the studio. I probably could have gradually acquired furniture, a bed here, a couch there, slowly moving onwards and upwards at work and, eventually, I would probably have been fairly satisfied. I would have had a life that I could have been proud to call my own, a life that many people would have been proud to call their own. If I didn't try to push past that, though, I knew I would never forgive myself, so I applied for a great-sounding job in another state. I felt it would be fitting to start fresh in an entirely new environment – a chance to put into practice everything I had learned since leaving the cult, away from the area I had grown up in and which, until now, had always had a hold on me. I wanted to prove that I could make it anywhere.

The way I saw it, I didn't have anything to worry about – I didn't know if I would get the job, but there was nothing to lose by applying. Either it would work and I'd be given the role, or I wouldn't get the job and I could go on and try something else instead. It wasn't the only option open to me; it was just the option I was focusing on for a brief moment in time. The important thing was trying, as is the way with so many aspects of life.

Shakespeare wrote that 'our doubts are traitors and make us lose the good we oft might win by fearing to attempt.' Well… Our doubts might not always be traitors as they can sometimes come from reason and logic (and they can, in fact, sometimes help us by reminding us that we need to protect ourselves from harm, instead of plowing into something we're unsure of at full speed), but there is some truth in those words. You never know what you might achieve if you only give it a try. If you put your fears aside and make an attempt, you might ultimately end up with a lot of good as a result. I worry that too many people hold themselves back because they're concerned about the bad that *might* happen, rather than the good that can come out of life. We sometimes forget that even though we might not always succeed when we attempt new things, if we don't even try them in the first place then we will definitely never succeed. So much of life is simply about believing in yourself and giving things a go, in choosing a goal and doing everything in your power to make sure you reach it. By having something important to aim for, to strive for. It's what I've done ever since I left the cult.

In my particular case, I did get a good result from my gamble. I got the job I had applied for, a position that required me to relocate from Pennsylvania. In the first instance, that had been one of the things that had attracted me to the job; relocating meant I would be breaking out of the mold I found myself in and that I would be much closer to my brother who lived in DC, something that was very important to me. If I could put physical distance between myself and the cult, I saw that as yet another way of moving forwards, another step along the path.

It had, however, taken the employers so long to get back to me about whether or not I had got the job, that my circumstances were somewhat different to the way they had been when I initially made my application. I suppose I shouldn't have been that surprised it took them six months to get back to me to let me know one way or the other. You can never predict how long things will take.

Six months, though. A lot can happen in six months. A lot *did* happen in six months.

In the time between submitting my application and getting the call to tell me I had been successful, I met someone. It had always been vaguely in my plans that one day, I would like to meet someone and eventually settle down with them. I just hadn't banked on it being so soon, or at that point in my life. Everything I was doing at that time was focused on my most basic of needs: shelter, food and family. I worked so I could eat and keep a roof over my head, and so I could get one step closer to seeing my brothers again. I had barely even considered the prospect of romance or anything like it. It had simply been the last thing on my mind.

It's funny how everything you've planned and everything in your life can be completely turned upside down in an instant, just because you meet a single person. I met him in 2006, when I was still in my early twenties. The relationship progressed quickly and I enjoyed the company of both him and his child, who he had from a previous relationship. He gave me a feeling of belonging and I felt like a new family – one that I made on my own, away from how I had previously lived – was now a distinct possibility.

Falling for someone so suddenly is quite strange. It flips your priorities on their head without warning. It changes your focus and I suppose that's a good thing. I had spent so long hell bent on nothing but survival; it had been consuming me for years. I sometimes found it hard to focus on anything other than how I was going to get through the next day, the next week, or where my next meal was coming from. Meeting this person made my life much more about the wonderful act of living, instead of just surviving and getting by in any way I could. It made me focus on something and someone outside my immediate sphere of interest. It meant I could stop worrying about simply existing and start actually living my life.

That was the reason it was harder when I finally got the phone call, telling me I had been successful with getting the job in another state. I hadn't known my boyfriend long, but I knew that I didn't want to leave him and his child behind. I liked the relationship we had and I didn't want to lose it. I would have felt selfish, simply disappearing out of their lives as quickly as I had arrived, without even offering them the chance to come with me in the hope of bettering their lives, too. My cousin had offered me a helping hand when I most needed it, and now I was doing the same for them.

To solve the problem, my boyfriend and I decided to get married. We did this to make it easier for all of us to relocate but we also did it because of love, and you should never get married without love. Love can, ultimately, make things so much harder in the long run – because it makes it hurt so much more if things don't go quite as you might have hoped, and it can make you stay in situations that logic tells you it would be better to leave – but it is still a vital feature of any relationship. We shouldn't let it blind us, but we should never be blind to it. It isn't news to say it, but it never hurts to remember its value: love makes you cherish the most mundane of things, from the tiny things like sharing a cup of coffee together while sitting on the couch to the bigger decisions such as where you're going to live for the rest of your lives. All of those essential things that are so necessary, so ordinary, love can transcend. It certainly did with me.

So we decided to marry, relocate together, and, with his son, become a little family of three.

I felt like I'd be starting over in more ways than the obvious, though. Even after I had left the cult, I had continued to live in its shadow. It was always still there, barely out of sight, like something you see flickering in the corner of your eye, just out of focus. Getting married would provide a break from that. It would represent the point where I severed my ties with my old life completely and made a new family for myself, making it an even bigger step than is usual for marriage. My path was being filled with more footprints, and they weren't just mine. Yet I felt ready and as though it was the right thing to do. The haze I had been living in for the past couple of years started to lift and I began to genuinely look forward to the life that lay ahead of me: as wife and mother and employee. It was all there for the taking, and those few brief moments – of waiting on the brink before I stepped over from one life into the next – offered the sweetest suspense I think I've ever known.

I was going somewhere. I felt like I could go anywhere. Do anything. Be anyone.

Through all of this, I kept thinking about my mother. I spent a lot of time trying to decide whether or not I should tell her that I was due to relocate and wondering how much I should say to her about my new life. Should I tell her about my soon-to-be husband and step-child? Should I introduce them? Would she be pleased to meet my new family if I did? Would it hurt her?

In the end, the decision was taken out of my hands; I was still vaguely in touch with some people from the cult and I heard through them that my mother was very ill. It had been going on for a while and she was on something of a downward slope. And, of course, because of the religious views of the cult, she wasn't allowed to go to the hospital to get help, so she just got steadily worse and worse – without any hope of getting better again.

Sometimes, I wonder what she thought during that time. I wonder if she accepted it, accepted the fact that she wasn't allowed to seek medical help no matter what happened, or whether, really, she wished that she could. I don't think it's uncommon, especially. Lots of people are stubborn about going to see the doctor all through their lives and will resist it at any costs, yet an extreme illness can be the shock they need to realize just how much they want to live and to make them seek the help they need. We all want to live: the survival instinct is humanity at its most basic level.

At any rate, my mother didn't seek help for her illness and so I chose not to tell her about the fact I was leaving. I didn't want to add any more stress or worry to her situation and telling her my news would undoubtedly not have helped. Before I moved states, though, I saw her two more times.

***THEY* MADE ME DO IT**

The first time I saw her before I left, I did what I probably should have done on that Thanksgiving day when I refused to take out my earrings at my father's request: I went over without wearing any jewelry and without any make up on. I also wore a long skirt, as was expected of women in the cult. It hurt to look at my mother. She was so weak and in so much pain, all I wanted to do was to pick her up and take her to the hospital. I was reminded of that time in my childhood, when my brother was dying in his room and my elder brother took him to the hospital against the wishes of our father. I wished I could do the same with my mother, but in a way, I think that would have been a violation. She had committed so much to the cult and that way of life that it would be almost cruel to take her away from that. I knew she certainly wouldn't have thanked me for it.

So instead, I just spent some time with her – playing hymn after hymn on the piano for her – soaking up our precious moments together and pretending that everything was normal. I'm not sure whether I was pretending for her sake or for my own, but to acknowledge or try to discuss the situation that we found ourselves in never really felt like an option. The whole thing felt very final, as though this chance wouldn't come again.

The second time I saw her before I relocated was at her funeral.

ELLE BENÉT

It's hard to say what I felt during that time, or how I felt at the funeral; I didn't really feel very much of anything. I knew that it was what my mother had wanted, that she had died how she had probably always expected to. It was something you were always aware of, in the cult, with its lack of belief in medical care and its focus on religion and making it to Heaven after death. I also knew that her death meant she was finally free: she wouldn't have to suffer anymore. She wouldn't have to go through her days working hard. She wouldn't have to worry any longer about my brothers and I, and what we might be going through. She was free now, like me. I was glad about that, and, as such, her death was more of a release than a cause for sadness. I still think this, even after so many years.

I suppose part of me felt like that because I hadn't exactly had a normal relationship with her. My mother was absent from my life long before she died. I know she loved me, I know she raised me as best she knew how and I know she overcame lots of struggles during my childhood. Despite all this, my craving for some simple maternal love went largely unfulfilled, because even though she was clearly packed full of love for all her children, she never really properly shared it. She couldn't, not with the way she lived – the way we were all expected to live. She never learned how to. The absence of my parent was already there, within me. Her death didn't exacerbate it. If anything, it helped, because it meant there was less room for fresh pain to be caused. I could simply remember her as best I could. I didn't have to worry about her anymore. It made me – and my brothers – so much freer.

My brothers were at the funeral, too. They didn't cry and so I didn't either. I wanted to be strong, just like them. I think that was the point when I finally realized that actually, I *am* strong. I didn't cry simply because I wanted to be like my brothers, I didn't cry because I was already like them. I was already strong, just like they are. I didn't need to fake it or put on an act. I was already there. I'd been there for a long time, partly because I didn't have any choice – if I wasn't strong then I would clearly have faltered long before – but also partly because it was already there, within me. The trials I'd been through in my life and the impact that my mother and my father had both had on me, the combination of all of it, meant that I was already strong. It had just taken me a while to see that in myself. I saw it at the funeral.

I think that ultimately, that's the biggest gift she gave me; without her I would certainly be weak. Largely unwittingly, she gave me the tools I needed to make it on my own and to face whatever it was that life decided to throw at me. She had done her job as a mother. Standing there with my brothers at her funeral, I absorbed that fact. Then I turned and looked forward to my new life, with my new family and my new job, in a new place away from all this.

Of course, it was a sad day in some ways, but it was also the start of the next part of my life. The next section of my path.

I have never been back to my mother's grave. I don't need to go there to remember her.

The next phase of my life was perhaps more traditional than anything that had happened to me so far. I married my boyfriend and we moved with his child to another state in 2007, where I started my new job. We quickly gathered the trappings of a life. We found somewhere to live and started to explore the neighborhood. My new husband worked as a personal trainer, and because of this, he was able to relocate his job to our new area and soon started work, too. We even bought a puppy, Sasha, to complete our little family. My goal of being successful and happy was getting ever nearer. My footprints were getting more solid as I continued along my path. It was nice and comforting to have our own little unit – husband and wife, child, and a dog. It felt safe.

For a short time, everything was as it should be. I had the nuclear family, the burgeoning career, a place to live… The future I had once found it so hard to imagine was beginning to materialize and I looked forward to discovering what would happen next. The thought of tomorrow was no longer frightening – it was exciting. I could see everything falling into place ahead of me and it felt like all the hard work I had put in over the years was beginning to pay off. The rewards were starting to come my way, finally. I'd spent so long just chipping away at things, working as hard as I could yet seemingly only making tiny amounts of progress at a time, and then suddenly, here it was, all together at once. I'd arrived.

I think there's something important to take from that. I've spoken to lots of people over the years who have felt like they were getting nowhere, no matter how hard they were trying. They work hard and do everything that they can to improve their lives, but still they feel as though they're stuck. They look at the path they've been walking along and realize it's seemingly hit a dead end. I have been one of those people. I've wondered what the point of it all is when you put in so much effort to get hardly anything back.

Well, let me tell you. It's the little victories that can sometimes make the big differences. It's the days when things are the slightest bit better at the end than they were at the start that make it all worth it. I know that these days can sometimes be few and far between. In some ways, it's much easier to go to bed in a worse mood than you woke in. It's so easy to think 'tomorrow will be better – I'll sort it out then. It's easy, but it doesn't necessarily get you anywhere. The problems will still be there in the morning, just as present in your mind as when you went to bed. It's the fights you fight today, so that tomorrow will be better, that make you feel the best. That make everything worthwhile.

I knew all of this when I relocated. I knew there was no point in putting off the inevitable; it would only hurt more in the long run. I knew that while facing a fight head on might not always be the best course of action, in a lot of ways it is better than leaving things to fester.

And yet, despite this, I did leave things to fester. The happiness and satisfaction I had found in those first few months after relocating were short lived. I guess I just didn't want to admit that things weren't completely right, at which point a kind of torpor set in and it became harder and harder to do anything about it. I began to understand why my mother had found things so hard, why she had never really fought for herself in all of the years that she was with my father. It's so easy to pronounce solutions when you're on the outside looking in, but as soon as it's your situation that is in crisis, it's suddenly much more difficult. It's harder to be objective about your own life: you're the one who has to live it, and to live with the consequences if you decide to make a change. The responsibility is solely on you.

***THEY* MADE ME DO IT**

The first crack in my new life began when I thought my husband might be having an affair. Just the thought of it left me feeling cold; we had only recently pledged to spend the rest of our lives together, so why would he do this? I thought this was it. We had committed ourselves to each other and the new life we shared. We had made plans. He had moved with me and his child to a new state. He had just as much invested in our relationship as I did, if not more. It seemed unfathomable that he would risk throwing it all away so soon by sleeping with someone else behind my back.

I tried not to believe it. Then, when it got to the point where I *had* to believe it, I tried to ignore it. I tried to pretend that the problem didn't exist. Admitting that I knew what was going on would just have been too hard, a battle which I wasn't yet ready to face, and, anyway, I didn't have any concrete evidence to prove what he was doing. For everything that I suspected, I knew he'd be able to deny it if he put his mind to it. Suspicious emails to female clients, absences when he should have been at home, money going out of our account… It was certainly all questionable, but not quite enough for a full-on guilty verdict. Not quite enough to give up on us.

Around the same time, I experienced a miscarriage. To date, it is one of the very worst things that has ever happened to me. I had been thrilled to find out I was pregnant. It was as though our little family was really starting to come together and I thought that the baby would complete the jigsaw puzzle as the last piece. I had already started imagining the child it might become, and the happiness it would bring with it. Losing it was awful. The baby may not have been old enough to survive outside my body – or well enough even to survive inside me – but it was still my child. Still my baby. Still my hopes and dreams. They say that losing a child is the worst thing that can happen to you and I think that's right. Not even getting the chance to know that child first made the whole thing even worse. It never even got a chance to live.

I tortured myself for ages afterwards, imagining what it would have been like to feel the baby growing and moving inside me and wondering what it would have been like when it was born. Would it have been a boy or a girl? What would I have called it? What color would I have painted the nursery?

All of these wonderful things that I had been planning for – bringing up a child, pushing them in the pram, holding them while they slept – had been taken away from me in an instant, and I felt the loss keenly. I still do. It created a gap inside me that I didn't think would ever close – a space that should have been filled by a tiny, warm life. I didn't have anyone to talk to about it, no source of support I could lean on to help me begin to heal and get over the loss. I couldn't even talk to my husband about it: I was still feeling betrayed about him having an affair and I didn't feel I could raise the issue with him. I suppose I didn't think he should get to see that part of me when he was so blatantly disregarding our commitment to each other. Opening up to him like that was not an option when he was clearly hiding so much from me. I didn't want to be vulnerable in front of him. I didn't want to seem powerless.

I suppose it's only fitting that what helped me get over the miscarriage in the end was another baby; I got pregnant again within a few months and, although I was ecstatically happy, I was also so nervous that something was going to go wrong for a second time. Although it was exciting to be growing a new life, I was still a bit apprehensive that something bad was going to happen again and take that chance away from me; however, the pregnancy proceeded just as I'd hoped. I spent months with my fingers crossed, watching the changes in my body, feeling the baby start to move within me and hoping against all hope that nothing would stop this baby from being born.

Once it became clear that – this time – it was going to work out fine, and once I began to feel more confident in my pregnancy, I started turning my attention once again to the future. I started to think about what would happen when the baby was born and wondering how my life would proceed from that point onwards. Would our marriage make it?

In May 2008 I ended up walking out on my husband. I still had that strong suspicion that he was cheating and I felt like I had to go. As far as I could see, he had violated our relationship and what we had together, and since it didn't seem as though anything was about to change, I left. The thing was, I didn't really have anywhere to go. Plus, of course, I was pregnant, which is hardly the best time to be trying to strike out on your own and wash the scars of the past away. Your body produces hormones when you are pregnant that are supposed to help bond you to the father of your child and I think that was part of the reason I didn't stay away. I went back to him before too long.

Maybe it was weak of me, but I didn't just have myself to think about anymore. I had to think about the baby and the stability of the life it would require: it would need to be provided for, and being on my own wouldn't be practical for that. I also wanted my baby to have a normal upbringing, the kind of upbringing I never had. My husband and I were planning on buying a house in a few months and it seemed foolish to walk away from all that; away from all of the plans we had made. I pushed all my doubts about him out of my mind and decided to give our marriage another shot, for the sake of the child.

***THEY* MADE ME DO IT**

I wasn't sure at all whether I wanted him to be present in the house when we bought it, but I felt as though I owed our family another chance at trying to make it work. Besides, I still couldn't decisively prove that he was having an affair, and while there was still reasonable doubt in my mind – even the slightest hint of doubt – I could convince myself that we were okay. Things would surely get better.

After that, I used to lie awake at night, just as I had done some nights living in my little studio apartment, wishing I could be somewhere else. I used to pray that I could get away from the marriage and start again, make things better and offer the best possible life to my unborn child. I'm not sure whether I was praying to God or just the strength I know is within me, but it gave me something to hold onto. It let me know that my options weren't closed, that just because I had come back this time, it didn't mean I had to stay forever.

The birth of the baby turned my world upside down, in the best possible way; the first time I held my daughter was one of those miraculous experiences that you read about but don't really believe until it actually happens to you. Here was this tiny human, completely dependent on me, and absolutely trusting in my abilities to do right by her. It's a powerful feeling – and a humbling one. To this baby, I was her entire world. To me, she was my whole world, too. It's one of those things that lets you know that power is only fleeting and that whatever grasp you have on the world, whatever understanding you may think you have of it, it can all be altered in an instant. I never knew I could love something this much. It was simply overwhelming.

It made my husband's infidelity seem that much smaller, if only because I suddenly had something so much better to focus on. My daughter was something good, something much more important than what had been going on between me and my husband. I wonder sometimes what he made of it all back then, if he had felt his world shift as much as I had mine. He must have. After all, he already had one child: he already knew the impact of it.

Despite that, my relationship with my daughter felt like a very private thing. I felt like it was just her and me against the world. I knew that no matter what happened, the two of us would be staying together and so my every responsibility was centered on her. She and I were the family that really mattered now.

The following year, I had another child – this time, a son – and my little family grew even more. That experience was similarly mind-blowing. Suddenly I was a mother of two babies and, even though they didn't know it, they helped me so much just by being there. They still do. No matter what happens, as long as they are there for me,

THEY MADE ME DO IT

I have a reason to fight. I love them more than words can say and all I want is for them to be safe and happy. Watching them grow up is the biggest pleasure I will ever know. They're still young enough that their personalities are still developing and it's amazing to watch them acquire new facets of themselves and discover new things about life. They are always learning, always gaining knowledge. The world is still wondrous and exciting to them, and I feel like it is to me as well, seeing it through their eyes. Their enthusiasm for learning about the world – something I was more or less denied in the cult – constantly amazes me.

It's commonly said that youth is wasted on the young and that parenthood is a second chance to do it all again and experience it as you should have done way back when. There's definitely something in that. Even with the endlessly bad TV shows that children seem to watch these days, there really is nothing like the discovery of youth, and doing it all over again as an adult is just incredible. For me, it has been even more amazing. Without a regular upbringing and without many of the simple pleasures of childhood, I feel like I'm doing a lot of it for the first time. Sometimes it makes me sad – that I missed out on so much of this during my actual childhood – but I think I appreciate it much more now than I would have done back then. I see how much it means to my children, how happy it makes them, and I love that I can share it with them. It is now my main mission in life to make sure my kids have the happiest childhood possible and that they always look back on these early years fondly, and not with regret. The lesson there is to enjoy it while you can, no matter how old you are.

February 14th 2010: Valentine's Day. The day I came face to face with the truth. It put an end to any and all suspicions and questions that had been rolling around in my mind regarding my husband's possible indiscretions. I got what I had been looking for right back in the beginning, before the children were even born: evidence. It was all right there – love letters, flowers, receipts – all sent to another woman. This time, there was no running from the decision that had to be made.

It was the support unknowingly given to me by my children that gave me the courage to finally leave my husband. I knew it was going to have to happen sooner or later; I could only ignore his affair for so long before I cracked and gave in to the desire to leave and get as far away from him as possible. In a way, I suppose it was similar to when I left the cult: it simply got to the point where I couldn't stay any longer. Would I have done it without the children there? I don't know. Probably, but I imagine it would have been more dragged out and probably would have hurt a lot more. With them there, I had a reason to pick myself back up – and fast.

Thinking back on it, it wasn't so much the fact that my spouse cheated on me with another woman that stung – while it hurt, I found it much worse that I had put my trust in him and he had let me down. Faith and trust are such important things. I don't give them lightly, and he had taken the faith I had in him, had taken my trust, and had betrayed it in the worst possible way. I still loved him, which made my decision to leave that much harder to make, but ultimately I knew that the situation couldn't continue. Back in the cult, even though I loved my mother, I had to leave for my own good. It was a similar thing with my husband. Even just thinking about what might happen further down the line and how it might affect the children inspired me to leave. I knew it would be hard for them, but I hoped the fact that they were still so young and would likely have little memory of this by the time they grew up might make it slightly easier for them to bear. So on that Valentine's Day, I told him that it was over and that I wanted a divorce.

So much changes when you divorce someone, and yet at the same time, so much stays the same. While certain parts of my life carried on as normal – work, the children – other parts were turned completely upside down. There was the painful task of dividing up the life we had made together and initiating changes to accommodate the separation we had just gone through, and unfortunately, that included our beloved dog, Sasha.

Sasha was a black and white cocker spaniel. She was tiny and full of energy, and I had loved her ever since we bought her, back when we first got married. After I left my husband, I cared for her as well as the children. I used to get up before 4:30am to let her out for her exercise, and then get myself dressed before getting the babies ready to go to daycare. Our hectic schedule meant that Sasha was often home alone for hours on end and, as much as I loved coming home to a happy, loving creature at the end of every day, I knew that the situation wasn't fair to her. She wasn't getting the attention she wanted and needed. She wasn't living the life she deserved to be living, and I could definitely relate to that.

It meant that I had to make a hard decision. I spent a while ignoring it, more so because the children and I loved her so much, but eventually I knew I had to do something about it. I couldn't carry on leaving her on her own for so long. I knew that if I really loved her, I should love her enough to know when I had to give her up. And now, it was time.

But knowing this didn't make it any easier; she was part of the family, and the thought of giving her up to go and live with someone else was really heartbreaking, even though

I knew that she deserved more time and attention than I could ever give her.

It was only when two of my brothers came to visit us one weekend that I finally dealt with the situation. I told one of them about the struggle I was going through, knowing that I should give Sasha up for her best interests but unable to bring myself to actually go through with taking her to the pound. As soon as I finished speaking, one of my brothers said, "I'll go with you." I think he knew that this was something I couldn't do on my own.

I didn't give myself any more time to think about it in case I changed my mind. I collected together Sasha's papers and then went with my brother to the pound. I had to do it all very quickly, before I managed to talk myself out of the whole thing, again like the time I left the cult. I think the staff there knew that I didn't want to give her up. "We'll take very good care of her," the woman who ran the place told me. "We don't put any animals down."

While I was relieved to hear that she would be well taken care of, it didn't do anything to dispel the sickening feeling I had in my stomach. I handed Sasha over to the lady, but I couldn't bring myself to say goodbye. I simply turned and walked away towards the door. I knew the dog would be following my every move, wondering where I was going, wondering when I would be coming back…

I heard Sasha start to whimper as I left but I couldn't bring myself to turn back to face her. I was crying inside, too, my heart breaking along with hers as my brother and I climbed back into the car, leaving her behind for good.

Sasha was one of the best things to come out of my marriage, and giving her up was one of the worst aspects of my divorce. I had to keep telling myself that this was a new phase in my life; I had to suppress my feelings about giving her up so that I could keep going and make it all work for myself and my children. If I start to reflect on the negative things, all of those memories will start to flow back in – and that's when I'll break down. If I do that, I won't be any use to my children, or any use to myself.

Once again, I found myself using the skills I had learned during my time in the cult: suppressing my feelings is something I'd been taught to do while growing up, and I started to find that I could apply these abilities – that may have been used in a negative way when I was younger – to my current life and the new and difficult situations I now had to face. I was becoming very adept at turning negatives into positives, even when life was seemingly heading – temporarily – in the wrong direction. I just had to find a new goal, a new target to strive for, for both me and my children.

THEY MADE ME DO IT

The day after I told my husband I was leaving, I went into work as normal. Getting back into a regular routine as soon as you can after a shock is meant to help things. It lets you know that life isn't over and that you can carry on through anything. I thought that if I kept going to work as I always did, it would take my mind off the things that were going on around me.

It didn't really work. I just kept thinking about everything; it was all going round and round in my mind and I couldn't stop it. I kept thinking of my mother, of all those times I had stood and watched her cry while I was growing up, of all those times I had watched her deal with everything on her own, effectively bringing up the children as a single parent. Suddenly, I saw myself in her shoes and reflected in my current situation.

Had things really changed so little that I had ended up just like that, despite my best efforts not to?

Or is it that, actually, no matter how you choose to live your life, a lot of the struggles are simply the same? Just because I vastly prefer life outside the cult to the way life was lived in it, it doesn't mean that 'out here' is perfect. There's rot everywhere. It made me realize that there is no quick solution to anything and, indeed, that there is no *perfect* solution to anything. That's okay, though. It means there's always room for improvement – room to learn and to grow – and that is no bad thing.

At the time, though, when I was having breakdowns at work and I was unable to stop these flashbacks of my mother, it certainly felt like a bad thing. I was lucky, really, to have a job where I was supported by my colleagues and to be working with people who cared about me. I didn't realize then just how much they did help, largely just by being there for me.

My boss suggested that I should seek therapy because there was no way I could deal with everything on my own and that I should, at the very least, find someone to talk to. That's something I find hard, though – opening up – and I think it was why it hurt so much that my husband betrayed me. It takes a lot for me to put my trust in someone and let them see everything about me, so having that trust thrown back in my face is one of the very worst things I could imagine. It still is.

This – the crying, the flashbacks and the breakdowns – went on for three days. Then one day I just looked at my kids and I thought *no more*. I couldn't afford to be like that anymore, not when they were there, depending on me, so sweet and innocent and everything that I needed.

***THEY* MADE ME DO IT**

Living in the cult made me very good at hiding how I feel, at keeping my emotions inside of me rather than letting them all out. It made me very good at dealing with things on my own. So that's what I did. I decided that I wasn't going to cry about my divorce anymore and so I didn't. My children have had a huge impact on me: they have taught me how to release all the emotion that I was never allowed to show during my own childhood, but they have also taught me how I can still be strong even with that emotion. It's not the weakness I was always taught it was. I had to get myself back together. Get myself back on the right path.

The next day, I went back to work. I was absolutely fine.

The night is ticking by and I wonder if I should sleep. Not yet, I tell myself. Not yet. You're too close to the end to stop now. Just keep going a little bit longer.

WHEN LIFE GIVES YOU LEMONS...

The divorce was undoubtedly a trying time in my life, but I refuse to be saddened by it now because of the good that ultimately came out of it. I have two wonderful children from that marriage, and they have brought a level of joy into my life that I never imagined possible. The divorce also freed me; it took me away from something that was holding me back and causing me pain, and it made me realize what I can do and what I can achieve in difficult circumstances. In that way, I felt similar emotions to those I'd experienced when I left my parents' house and, in turn, the cult: the words 'freedom' and 'liberation' immediately come to mind. I didn't have to worry about my marriage any longer, just as I hadn't needed to worry about the cult any longer, or about my mother when she passed away. I could go on and live my life how I wanted to live it without trying to please everyone else. More than anything, it was a relief.

I already knew that I could be strong, but this time, having the children relying on me instead of having just myself to look after, it mattered so much more that I should succeed and come out the other side of the difficult time. I won't lie and say it was easy, because it definitely wasn't. There were times when I faltered, when I was unable to deal with things as I would have liked to have done, but I managed. Giving up Sasha was horrible, especially when all I wanted to do was keep her, but I knew that I had to do it. It made me see that I am not selfish; I loved her completely, but I also loved her enough that I could let her go in order for her to have a better life.

I knew I'd been strong enough to leave the cult and make it on my own, and now I knew that I was also strong enough to go through a divorce and give up my current way of living – as well as my beloved dog – and still come out of the other end being stronger than ever. My experience with the cult had prepared me for my experience with the divorce, and it was to prepare me for even more things to come in my life. For this, I am grateful for everything I had to go through when I first moved out of my parents' house and in with my brothers; that extremely difficult time in my young life had set me up for this one, and extremely successfully so. I was able to deal with it in a much better way than I would have been able to at age 18. My life skills were building up, and they were serving me well. I have the cult to thank for my strength of character, and for making me realize that no matter how hard things seem to get, I won't let myself give up.

And, perhaps the most important thing of all, I had people there for me, people who supported, helped and guided me – my colleagues and my brothers and, last but not least, my babies. The presence and endurance of that support network has to be one of the best things to come out of that whole trying period of my life, and for that, I am extremely grateful.

CHAPTER FOUR

Even though it was largely for the sake of my children that I left my husband, I still hesitated over it – because of them as well. I knew that leaving him effectively meant becoming a single parent. I would have to cover all of their day-to-day needs, without any of his help. I'd have to be their sole provider. I would, essentially, have to assume the same role that my own mother had.

This led to practical challenges: it meant I would have to work longer hours in order to meet the mortgage and day care payments. It meant I would have to balance my time that much better in order to be around when they needed me. It meant I would have to make personal sacrifices in order to pick up the slack when my husband was no longer around, and to make sure I still spent as much time with the children as I could. It's a hard fact about being a single parent; the children can so often end up seeing less of both parents as the one looking after them has to work harder and longer to keep a roof over their heads, at a time when kids need their parents more than ever. I was determined that my children wouldn't have to go through that; they would still have their mother there as much as possible. This was very important to me.

It also led to the obvious emotional challenges. I found myself wondering whether I could be a single parent, whether I would be enough for my children on my own. I wondered what I would do, where I would turn to, if I felt like I needed some support. I wondered how it would affect my children, and what I would do if it seemed as though they were suffering.

Overall, though, I concluded that the positives of the situation outweighed the negatives and that I would be able to meet any challenge that was thrown at me. The kids and I would be fine without my husband, their father, as long as we had each other. It was sink or swim. And while I'm not much of a swimmer, I've always had enough determination and drive to keep my head above the water, so in the end, I wasn't afraid of taking the plunge. This is why I am still feeling so confident, years after the divorce, despite the things that came next. I knew that I would survive – the kids, too.

One of the main things that had alerted me to my husband's affair was his justifications of business purchases when there was a mortgage that needed to be paid. "We'll catch up next month," he would tell me. "No need to worry." As a result of me wanting to trust him, and him spending money we didn't have on someone who wasn't me or the children, we ended up getting behind on our mortgage. I still ponder whether it was to disconnect himself from the mortgage note, but after he was confronted in February about his affair, he readily turned over the house to me.

I applied for workout assistance, a package of support from a financial institution that would let me meet the mortgage payments on my own. I submitted all of my documents in February 2010 and I felt really positive that my children and I would be okay. Soon we would be set up on our own, in our new lives, ready to move forwards again. Ready for the next step. I had done everything correctly, in good faith, and I was confident that we would get a good decision as there was no decent reason to turn down my application for support. I had followed the right processes and taken action as soon as I knew I needed to.

Unfortunately, the mortgage industry doesn't have a soul, or if it does, it doesn't have much of one. It doesn't tend to see people as people; it sees them as documents and cold, hard cash. I'm sure anyone who has ever had a mortgage – or any significant dealings with the industry – will understand. Even if they are giving you the result that you want, it's still hard to believe in it.

I heard nothing from the bank after sending them my package. When I got in touch with them to find out what was going on, they told me they'd never received it. So I tried again. These things happen sometimes, after all. It could have been a genuine error, the package having been lost somewhere in transit. This time, in order to make certain my application was received, I made it a point to obtain a certificate of service.

Despite this, the same thing happened again – the bank told me they'd never received my package. "We never got it," they said. It can become rather frustrating when you're unsuccessful in following the procedures – *their* procedures – having done everything correctly. More than anything, I wanted it all sorted out. I just wanted to get back on track with my mortgage to ensure my children's home would be secure. I wanted to move on with my life, continue along my path. I wanted my children to be able to move on with me, without any worries or concerns whatsoever. Determined, I sent in my documents for a third time.

In June 2010, I was finally accepted for workout assistance. I was elated! It was a long time coming, but it meant ensuring a roof over my children's heads, so it was well worth the wait. It meant that we would be able to manage and make progress, which was just what I wanted. Moving forwards, as always, was very important to me. It felt like the kids and I were on the way to sorting ourselves out as a new little family unit. There are three bedrooms in our house and I felt like it was kismet – one for each of us.

THEY MADE ME DO IT

Unfortunately, my bliss was short lived when in August I received a letter from the bank saying we were facing foreclosure. This was despite everything I had sent them *three* times and the fact that they had sent me the letter of approval only two months before. Had I been accepted for workout assistance after all? I felt that they wouldn't have accepted and processed my check had I not been.

I don't know if you've ever been faced with foreclosure, but let me tell you, being informed – via a cold letter, no less – by someone with more power than you, that your home might be taken away from you, is truly awful. I'd worked so hard to do the right thing and this was what I received in return. I had no idea what was going on. I thought I had left all of the confusion and uncertainty behind me, and yet here it was, back again, so soon after I had finally put it to rest. Even the slightest possibility that our home might be at risk was frightening. Still, I kept it together for the children; they didn't need to know the seriousness of what was going on. I didn't want to burden them with any worry.

By September, I really didn't know what to do. I just couldn't see exactly how I was supposed to sort it out and, even after almost a year, the answer was still not clear. How does one person take on the entire mortgage industry? How do you take on even one branch of one bank? It isn't easy. And I was tired – so tired. I'd spent the past year working ten hour days at work so I could provide for my family. I was being both a mom and a dad to my kids. Everything was so stressful, all of the time. There was no break from it, at all. It was starting to affect my performance at work and I could feel myself slipping, something which I found hard to admit to myself.

Every day for a year, I had woken up in the morning and taken great care to put on my poker face before I stepped outside my bedroom door. I had to. After all, life goes on no matter how you're feeling on the inside. It doesn't stop just because you're feeling low or because you would rather stay in bed for the day. It meant that when I was laughing at someone's joke, they couldn't see that I'd actually rather be crying. It meant that when I was listening to people and giving them advice, they couldn't see that I was dying for some guidance of my own. Maybe I should've just let the mask slip, let someone in to help me, but old habits die hard. It was my protection, and I needed it. It's how I manage to keep going no matter what happens, and I was worried what would happen if I let my true feelings show. What if it meant I couldn't carry on any more? I promised myself I wouldn't let it get that far.

Everyone has a poker face, I think, but mine was starting to take more effort to maintain than most. The fact that I worked so hard and yet couldn't seem to guarantee my kids a roof over their heads was killing me. Every day was a performance: before I left my bedroom in the morning, I would take a minute to gather myself, to lock everything away deep inside me and steel myself to face the day, telling myself that I had to keep it together for the kids. They were my motivation. They deserve to be happy, and they shouldn't be worried about anything at their age. I wasn't going to put them through any of the fear and confusion I'd felt as a child, growing up in the cult. Telling myself that was how I kept my mask in place, but all the same, I knew it wouldn't take all that much for it to slip.

Eventually, I took a trip to see a close friend in California. I just needed to get away from it all and I thought the distance might offer a little perspective, in which I might find the answers to my foreclosure problem; sometimes seeing things from a distance can help them make sense in a way that they didn't before. It also gave me the chance to drop my mask for a few days and indulge myself, so by the time I left I would be strong enough to face everything once again. I wasn't trying to run away from my problems; I just needed a little bit of space so I could think and recharge my batteries – as well as get some advice from a good friend. Such things really cannot be overestimated.

I told my friend everything that was going on with the bank and it felt so good to get it off my chest. They say that a problem shared is a problem halved and, while

I'm not completely sure I believe that, it definitely does help to be able to talk to someone you trust and who loves you. The problem was still there, but it was a relief to have someone else know what was happening, especially someone who was on my side. Even just telling my friend made me feel better and she was able to offer some sensible thoughts, which can be so hard to come by when you're so close to the fire. She said it was probably a simple error on the bank's part and that they hadn't realized the stress they'd been causing me. They had probably just made a small administrative error somewhere along the line that had then grown larger as they failed to notice and fix it. These things happen. When systems are so automated and computers regularly send out so many different types of letter as a matter of routine, they probably didn't even realize that something had gone wrong. It sounded plausible.

There's an argument there that they should definitely have been paying more attention to my case when the situation was so serious, but at that point I was just happy to have a logical, simple explanation that meant everything would be okay. It all made sense: I had been approved for workout assistance, so how could they be foreclosing on me? Someone had probably just forgotten to update some system or other, and that was why I was getting all these letters.

THEY MADE ME DO IT

I was certain that all I had to do was snap out of my current malaise and contact the bank about the discrepancy. It would be easy to solve. It had to be.

Eager to sort out the problem, I picked up the phone and called the bank, totally unprepared for what I was about to hear. The representative, after reviewing my files, pleasantly notified me that my house was set for sale within just a few days. I went from disbelief – thinking that there was no way that could possibly be the case – to sheer panic as I worried what me and my babies would do, where we would go, how we could stop it. Have you heard that expression about having the bottom drop out of your world? That's how I felt then.

Part of me knows that a house is only bricks and mortar, and that a house doesn't necessarily make a home, but that house really *was* our home. I had big plans for it. The thought of leaving there, of being thrown out through no fault of my own – for a *bank error* – was awful. I can't even describe it. I couldn't even let myself think the word 'homeless' because I knew that if I started down that path, I'd never get myself off it. I was angry, shaking, panicking. My friend had to medicate me to calm me down.

The representative on the phone had gone on to say that, actually, I had been denied for workout assistance because the signatures on the documents didn't match those on the original note that I had sent. It didn't make any sense. I told her that the documents had been notarized and were valid, and then, oddly enough, my phone call was disconnected. Like I said, they don't see people as people. They just see boxes that have to be ticked and targets that have to be met, and if you don't fall neatly into one of their categories, then sorry, but you're on your own. For them, it's all about the bottom line. For me, my house was my bottom line. Without it, the children and I only had each other.

The chain of events that were taking place made me realize something: I don't think they ever meant to approve me for workout assistance. I think they were just biding their time until they could sell my house from under me and make some fast money. I hate to be so cynical – especially when I'd like to think that the industry must be staffed with people who have feelings and homes of their own – but I don't know what else to think about the whole thing. Can their administrative systems really be so bad that they would do such a thing otherwise? Well, maybe. But I also know how big corporations work. They have targets to meet and one of those targets is bound to relate to foreclosures. It isn't personal, at least not to them, but it's part of the job. I hope I'm wrong, I really do.

I decided, though, that there was no way I could just let them take me for a ride, if only because it wasn't just me they were messing with. If it *had* been just me, maybe I would have taken it, but I had the children to consider, too; it wouldn't just be me out of a home if the bank went through with their plans. How they could do such a thing to small children, I had no idea.

I spent the last two days in California researching everything I needed to know in order to file a lawsuit against the bank. It was too short a notice to try and find an attorney considering the kind of times in which I was dealing; I couldn't waste valuable days looking for a lawyer when my timescale for action was counted in just hours. As with many other things in my life, I would have to do it myself. My intentions were to be prepared to pick up my children and head to the court house to file my lawsuit as soon as my plane landed. And two days prior to the auction date of my home, I accomplished just that.

By this point, things were simply not adding up. I began making notes to pinpoint exactly what was causing the confusion. It went something like this:

1. Twice I submitted payments with the workout assistance paperwork the bank required to be considered for assistance. Despite being told by the bank that the paperwork had never been received, the checks I had sent to them were cashed. It seemed, therefore, that someone, somewhere, actually *had* received the

paperwork, and had taken enough notice of it to see that there were checks in there that could be cashed. What happened to the rest of the paperwork, I have no idea.

2. I researched the statues pertaining to my state in order to better understand the procedure for auctioning off a homeowner's house. The bank had failed to mail any notification of their intent to auction off my home, as is required by the statutes. I had only discovered the sale upon *my* contacting *them* to clear up the discrepancy. They had failed in their duty to inform me of their intent.

3. The week after I filed my lawsuit I received two offer letters from the bank – on the last offer they even told me what my mortgage payment would be if I accepted their offer by a specific date. On what basis did they determine my mortgage note if they had no financial information from me to go on? After all, they claimed they'd never received any of my prior paperwork.

I took things a step further and began looking into signatures and dates on my loan since the financial institution bought the loan from another bank. What surfaced was astonishing: documents containing questionable signatures, an allonge that seemed to materialize out of nowhere, the same individuals signing under various titles. I was awestruck.

The weight of the pressure at work and the endless nights of research were taking a toll on my body – both physically and mentally. The stress had just become too much for me and I felt like the pressure in my head was about to erupt. I was tired and distressed and faced with endless information to digest so I could try and save our home. I was wishing there was some sort of pause button – something to stop the endless stream of questions and worries that were churning mercilessly through my mind. Had the sale gone through? What would happen to my children and me if it had? Where would we go if we were forced to leave our home? What would it make the children think? It all became too much and, finally, my body gave in to the pressure of what was happening. On 1 October I found myself in the emergency room.

I'm sitting in the dark. There are no windows, no discernible sounds or other distractions, nothing left to do but contemplate the things that happened to get me here. In an abstract sense, there are many people who could be held responsible for my current position – they made me do it. They all helped me, in their own way. Those who supported me as well as those who attempted to hold me back. Without them, I would never have done it.

But it's getting late. I can hear the timbers of my house creaking and feel the weight of the night bearing down around me, but it's not scary or oppressive. I like the dark. This is my life. This is where I live. My children are upstairs sleeping while I type this, and soon I will tiptoe up the stairs to press kisses to their faces before crawling into bed and awaiting the arrival of another day. I push my chair under my desk and close the door to my office.

For years, I was merely a larvae wrapped in a case that was spun by life's challenges; I had been hanging in suspended animation allowing experiences to develop and mold me. It was dark in there and I anticipated the day I would escape. And after 27 years, I finally emerge.

I am free.

THEY MADE ME DO IT

WHEN LIFE GIVES YOU LEMONS...

Fighting a foreclosure is not something I ever anticipated having to do. It's not something that's pleasant to think about, for anyone. While the circumstances that led up to it were particularly not pleasant to reflect upon- my husband's infidelity and the frustrating experience of applying for workout assistance- like everything else in my life, the experience has taught me an important lesson: it taught me that I can focus on anything I put my mind to. In the case of the foreclosure it was the intellectual challenge. I had to read and understand statutes without the help of an attorney – and in such a short space of time – in an effort to save the house. And presenting my own case before the courts was especially daunting. But on a positive note is showed me that I am prepared to do anything for my children, and that I won't just give up.

Through my investigation into the loan on my house, I uncovered questionable documents that might just help my case. It didn't fix the problem straight away, but it gave me the valuable evidence I needed. Once again, I had set my sights on the goal required, and I didn't back down or give in. I know that I will be as successful in event of my life. Leaving the cult, the miscarriage, the divorce, having to give up Sasha… everything has led me to this point: I'm stronger than I've ever been, and I will keep pushing on until the situation reaches its conclusion.

All of my experiences have taught me that life does not have to be an uphill battle. Life is meant to be enjoyed. When you find the perfect balance between persevering and letting go your load will lighten. I do not use "letting go" in the context of becoming deterred and thus "giving up" (because we must persevere of course). Letting go does not mean losing sight of your goals and dreams. When you let go and don't attempt to control the situation, you soon realize that the roadblocks you encounter in life are not roadblocks. They are simply detours, if you will. I liken it to traveling in a vehicle en route to your way home. You intend on taking a particular road only to find it's blocked off-but it doesn't mean you won't get home! There is more than one path to reach our destination. And the same applies for your journey in life. We must let go and accept that sometimes roads will be closed- but we must have enough willpower to persevere and believe that, though we may not use the road we *expected*, we *will* reach our goals.

When I set out to write this book, my aim was to show everyone that there is always hope – there is always a way through whatever life throws at you and there is always something positive to take from any experience. I trust that, if nothing else, the sense of that has come across. There is too much inherent good and happiness in life to allow yourself to be overwhelmed by the negative.

It's an unfortunate fact of life that 'bad' things, every now and then, do happen. Sometimes, they are things that happen because of our own actions – however unintentional – and other times, they just come out of the blue for no discernible reason. Sometimes, it seems as though the bad things just keep on coming.

Obviously, it's not a pleasurable experience when seemingly negative situations occur since stress and heartache usually ensue… but there is always tomorrow. There is always another day, and the hope that things will be better. I feel blessed that I have been able to overcome so much in my life so far. I'm proud that I've prevailed over all the challenges that have been thrown at me and I'm glad that I have learned so much from each and every experience.

For a long time, I wondered whether it was a good thing to be able to shut my emotions off so quickly, but the birth of my children made me realize that actually, yes, it *is* a good thing. It's not something that suits everyone, but it certainly suits me. If I didn't have the ability to move past things quickly, I would still be trying to get over my marriage. I wouldn't be the parent that I need to be for my children, because I would be spending too much time looking within myself instead of looking outwards, towards them. Of course, it is valuable to reflect, to make time for yourself and to deal with things – but you also have to do things in your own way. When there are other people who are depending on you, you have to learn how to put them first. My children need me to be happy and whole so that they can be, too, and if that means I have to hide some of my feelings from them, then so be it. I want them to always feel safe and know that I will always be here for them. I want them to have security.

I think that being able to shut off some of my emotions has also helped me get over the experiences I went through when living in the cult.

Growing up there has impacted my whole life, and it's still something that I think about regularly, but now I can consider putting that whole time behind me as one of my greatest achievements. Now, I can think about it as something that once was, but is no more in my life. I can remember the things that were good about my childhood – the love of my mother and my brothers, the possibility of what the future might hold. I can remember the negative aspects of cult life with the benefit of hindsight, and the other benefit of not having to live that life any longer.

I could so easily have let the experience of growing up in that environment overtake me and, in turn, succumb to it. I could have gone back there when things got difficult after my brothers and I moved out, or I could have let myself go to pieces out here, in the real world. Instead, I picked myself up and built a new life for myself from the foundation up. It hasn't been perfect, but life isn't meant to be perfect. I've set my sights on the future instead of dwelling on the past, and I think that's incredibly important. No matter how you choose to deal with your emotions – whether by shutting them down and moving past them, or getting them out in the open – you need to have one eye on the future, or else how are you ever going to get there?

My children have definitely helped me with that. They are so bright and vivacious, so full of life that I can't fail to be thrilled whenever I think of them. There will always be tomorrow while I have them and that thought fills me with more joy than I can ever express. My children have also given me the chance to live vicariously through them and experience the childhood I never had.

I am excited that there is still so much of my life yet to come. I am still young, and so are my children. The prospect of getting to watch them grow up, learn and slowly become the people they are meant to be is a lovely one. There is so much to look forward to, and they never fail to make me proud. There is so much more that I can do, too. I still have the time to achieve more. I can grow in my role as a mother, as well as in my career. I could go to college if I wanted. I could do a good deal of things, some of which I might not even have envisioned yet. Despite the challenges my family still face, there are so many possibilities, so many different, exciting opportunities, and so many good reasons to live in and be appreciative of this world.

Despite my father and I not seeing eye to eye, he attributed greatly to the dedication I exhibit to what I believe in and my ability to never lose sight of it. His faith and beliefs are solid, and he has taught me the value of truly believing in something, whatever that may turn out to be. When I watch him interact with his grandchildren, I recognize his efforts to better himself as a person and it makes me realize that anyone can change if they put their mind to it. He is getting better. I appreciate his willingness to create a more harmonious relationship with me – and while it won't amend the past, it *can* improve the future. After all… life is all about moving forwards, even if it is just one small step at a time.

I hope that my relationship with him will continue to improve, and it is nice to know that he is making the effort, that despite appearances all throughout my childhood and early adult life, he must truly care for his family. I may not agree with many of his beliefs and his general way of life, but his desire to do what he sees as right by his family is definitely something I can relate to. All I want is to do right by my children, so that they can have a better future. It's all any parent wants.

I have already decided that if – when they get older – my children discover this book and want to read it, I will let them. If they have any questions,

I would have no issues with responding to their inquiries. But I won't volunteer the details of my past to them; it is the person who I am now that is important to show them, not the girl I was at 10 years old or the woman I was becoming at age 18. I want to support my children in their exploration of the world – and their exploration of religion, if they choose to follow one of those paths – but I don't want to control them in the same way I was controlled, and I don't want them to go through anything alone. I want to grant them the opportunity to face and overcome challenges – but with my help and guidance.

Kismet has been mentioned a couple of times in this book, such as the time I met my cousin when I was in desperate need of somewhere to stay. I believe that these moments in my life are steps on the stairwell – or footprints on the path – that helped me to get to where I am today. I don't believe in coincidences; I believe that – based on our ultimate desires and goals – we emit an energy that attracts us to the avenues and paths that will help us get to our destination. Above all else, though, I believe in hard work and the ability to achieve in life whatever we set our minds to. I will be teaching my children that in their lives, they are only limited by the limitations they place upon themselves.

One thing that I learned in the cult that has never left me is the importance of structure within the family, and while I won't be subjecting my children to most of the things I experienced when I was growing up, I will try and instill that value of family within them. This can just be something as simple as sitting down and having dinner together, talking about our days and what's been happening at school. Gathering together as a family truly does bring unity, and I will remember that when raising my own children.

I now have the support network I always felt I was lacking growing up, too. I might still take pains to keep my poker face in place, but I also have people around who I know will always be there for me, no matter what. I didn't even realize many of them were there at first. I spent so much time feeling so alone that it's really only with hindsight that I feel I can say *yes, you helped me*. When you are in the midst of a personal crisis, it can be so easy to feel as though you are doing everything completely on your own and fail to miss the invisible support given by those around you. Now that I've emerged out of the other side and I recognize the contribution they made, I can't thank those people enough. There aren't many people like that, who will always be there no matter what and who can make things better just by being themselves, but everyone needs at least one person to fulfill that role for them. You probably already have someone, even if you don't know it yet. It often isn't until times of crisis that you know who they are, but if you do know who they are, make sure they know you love them because they will give you more than you will ever be able to repay.

My journey still isn't over. Sometimes I feel slightly apprehensive when I think about what might happen; although I have a great enthusiasm for the future, there is still so much uncertainty about what it might bring. I'm still fighting to keep my house and I guess you never know what might be thrown at you next. Despite this, I have never been more excited about the future. All the components for a good life are there: my kids, the house (fingers crossed), my job, my friends, my dreams – all of it. All of the pieces are there. Now I just need to put them together.

I have plans. It's good to have plans; it gives you something to aim for. I've heard it said that elderly people in residential homes live longer and are happier when they have plans, when they can still see a future for themselves, a list of things that they intend to complete, big or small. I, too, intend to keep on planning and dreaming right up to my dying day. Life would be pretty boring without those things. There is so much out there to do and to achieve, more than you could ever think possible, no matter where you come from or what journey you took to get to where you are now. Everyone's path is different.

I want to be a successful businesswoman. Actually, scratch that. I am *going* to be a successful businesswoman. I don't have it all perfectly worked out yet, but I know I have the ability and the determination to make myself the success I'm going to be. I want to be a good example to my children, someone they can look up to and admire. I want them to be proud of me, and I want them to look at me and see that it *is* possible to do what you want, that you can create your own success no matter what life happens to conjure up.

Success can be measured in so many different ways. In our society, we often measure it in terms of money – the more of it you have, the more successful you must be. We measure success by what we see on the outside; the classy outfits, the perfect house, the smiling children. Those things definitely matter; possessing my own house is one of my biggest achievements, something I've always wanted to do. My children, however, have to be my biggest success of all – I am so proud of the people they are becoming and they make me feel like I have done something really good for this world. They alone have been worth all the pain and stress of my earlier life and everything that has been thrown my way ever since.

But success isn't just about the visible things, the things that we can see and measure. It is also an intensely personal thing, measured according to our own private yardsticks and goals for ourselves. It is about how we feel inside. For instance, I see one of my big successes as remaining positive throughout my life, for always believing that things can improve. Often, it is so easy to be negative, and at several points along the way I could have succumbed to that negativity, but I didn't. This kind of success might not bring material riches, but it brings a wealth of valuable experience.

I am a happy, well-adjusted adult. When I consider the childhood I had, I think that this is an important success in and of itself. It makes me sad to think of those young people who left the cult full of dreams, only to end up back where they started, or else turning to a life of drugs and drink to numb the hurt and make life bearable. I could so easily have resorted to the same lifestyle, but I fought. I fought against that. I kept my determination to make a life outside of the cult and I did what I set out to do; I successfully put one foot in front of the other – even when it seemed almost pointless to do so – and I reached my goals. I achieved what I wanted to achieve.

I have come out on top. I have a positive attitude that gets me through every day. I believe that I can solve any problem life sends my way. I have a job I like and children I adore. On top of that, there is the potential for more success in the future. I'm so proud to have written this book, to have worked through things that have troubled me for a long time, to get them down on paper and to share my story with others. I hope that I can inspire people with the words written on these pages. I hope that people read them and know that they can always make things better, however bad they might seem in that moment. If I can do that – if I can inspire people – that will be a huge success on my part.

Writing this book has been therapeutic, and while this is the reason I started to put my life down on paper in the first place, it is not the most important thing about releasing this book. Reflecting on my past has been a cathartic experience for me (as

I'd hoped), but I won't go back and read the book afterwards. I liken it to the passing of my mother; I won't visit her grave because I don't feel I have to. I don't want to reawaken all the pain and begin reflecting on everything bad that happened, I want to remember the good parts and take those with me into the future – the most important thing to come out of my remembrances is that I can use them to sculpt the future, not dwell on the past. My main objective now is to help and inspire other people – whether they're in a similar situation or can relate to just a few aspects of my journey – and help them in making a better future for themselves. Once this book is released, it ceases to be about me and, instead, focuses on others out there who may be seeking guidance of their own. I'll always take the time to realize just how far I've come, but I will no longer dwell on my past. I will look forwards to the future – mine and others.

I have already started to help others with my story, and this is a privilege that I truly appreciate. Recently, I had a young man – who had grown up in the same community – reach out to me for guidance. He was struggling with the decision to leave the cult, much as I had, and he was having a particularly hard time dealing with the way his family would shun him because of his choice. The fact that I had left – and was successfully living outside of the cult without having given in to going back, or resorted to alcohol or drugs – had given him hope. That one single word is *so* important, and I am extremely happy that I have been able to give him this wonderful gift.

He also asked my advice on dealing with the outside world, and I let him know that the transition is difficult, but that it is more of a mental struggle than anything else. For years, I thought that when something bad happened to me – having no money, struggling for food – it was because of my decision to leave the cult. I thought I was being punished, but it just wasn't so. I told the young man that bad things do sometimes happen, and it is simply this thing called 'life'. I also told him that if he left and then decided to go back to the cult, there was nothing wrong with that as long as he was being true to himself – as long as he was doing it to satisfy himself and not because he wanted to appease his family. In the end, it is up to him to make up his mind, but with the knowledge and hope that my story has provided, I'm sure he'll make the decision that is best for him. That's all I ask.

My experiences have made me realize that we can create any life we want for ourselves. We start with so much potential, and ultimately, the only thing that can hold us back is ourselves. The human capacity for imagination and creation is immense. We all have the ability to dream; we just have to find the spark within us, that thing that inspires us to go for what we want and do whatever we can to achieve it. It might be the desire to start again somewhere new, or to have a family, to achieve in your career, go to college, learn a skill, or to simply carry on dreaming. It could be anything – anything that matters to you. We might not always be able to control the journey that takes us through our lives, but as long as we have our goals and our dreams, we'll get there in the end. We'll progress. We have a destination, and a determination to get there in one piece. We just have to find the path that will take us there.

I found my path. It may not have been the one I anticipated; it certainly wasn't perfect or straightforward and it was most definitely filled with surprises – both good and bad – but it was *my* path. I am grateful for having travelled along it, and for the destination it has helped me to reach.

After reading my story, you may well think that I'd have the right to blame people for what happened in my childhood, in my past, and in my recent present, but there simply isn't any point. I am proud of what I have achieved, proud of the things I have gone through, and proud of the strong individual I have become because of it all. I wouldn't have it any other way, and I will always be grateful for whatever life throws at me.

They made me do it, and I'm glad they did.

I hope this book inspires you to feel the same as you walk along your own personal path and towards your own bright future.

www.ingramcontent.com/pod-product-compliance
Lightning Source LLC
Chambersburg PA
CBHW032054090426
42744CB00005B/215